Tales from the Therapy Room

Praise for the book

These engaging, moving, informative, warm and surprising stories convey the key points in counselling and psychotherapy practice. Overall, a beautifully written book that should be a real asset to the counselling and psychotherapy literature.

Mick Cooper,
Professor of Counselling, University of Strathclyde

I've read each of these stories through several times, simply because to do so was a sheer delight. They are written with warmth and humour, and give a valuable insight into the world of therapy. Therapists regularly find themselves confronted with dilemmas and this book helps alert the reader to the importance – and everyday nature – of reflecting on these sorts of issues.

Mike Simmons,
University of Wales, Newport

The topics reflect aspects of our studies and give an insight into how these might be identified in real life. Anyone on a counselling course will be looking for a book such as this, to lighten up the heavy load of academic reading. It makes you think, as well as backing up your learning.

HNC Counselling & Psychotherapy student,
Anniesland College

As a student on a counselling course, I honestly thought this was the best book I have come across relating to therapy. The skills demonstrated by the counsellor were shown in short captivating stories that kept my attention throughout, meaning that I picked up more than I had in course handouts or from the reading list textbooks.

HNC Counselling & Psychotherapy student,
Anniesland College

Tales from the Therapy Room

Shrink-Wrapped

Phil Lapworth

Los Angeles | London | New Delhi
Singapore | Washington DC

SAGE Publications Ltd
1 Oliver's Yard
55 City Road
London EC1Y 1SP

SAGE Publications Inc.
2455 Teller Road
Thousand Oaks, California 91320

SAGE Publications India Pvt Ltd
B 1/I 1 Mohan Cooperative Industrial Area
Mathura Road
New Delhi 110 044

SAGE Publications Asia-Pacific Pte Ltd
33 Pekin Street #02-01
Far East Square
Singapore 048763

Library of Congress Control Number: 2010926691

British Library Cataloguing in Publication data

A catalogue record for this book is available from the British Library

ISBN 978-0-85702-494-7
ISBN 978-0-85702-495-4 (pbk)

Typeset by C&M Digitals (P) Ltd, Chennai, India
Printed in India at Replika Pvt Ltd
Printed on paper from sustainable resources

To Leo and Laurie

Contents

Acknowledgements

My grateful thanks to:

Charlotte Sills for having faith in my writing and for giving invaluable feedback.

Alice Oven, at Sage, for being so encouraging and for taking a risk.

Karnac Books for their kind permission to include 'Dream On' in this collection.

My clients for sharing with me their real stories and teaching me so much.

Introduction

Tales from the Therapy Room is a collection of 10 fictional short stories exploring aspects of the process of therapeutic work and the client–therapist relationship from the viewpoint of the therapist. The reader is invited into the therapist's experience and ways of working and given a 'fly-on-the-wall' view of the therapeutic endeavour. These tales aim both to entertain and to provide a door into the often-hidden perspective of what a therapist might think and feel within (and without) the therapy sessions.

This is not intended as a guidebook on how to do therapy. The stories depict one therapist's integrative way of working with a variety of clients, the experience he has, the thinking he does and the decisions he makes in his attempt to facilitate his clients' desire to understand themselves and bring about change through this unusual and unique relationship. I do not want to suggest a 'right' or 'wrong' approach to therapy but rather provide a starting point to explore a range of possibilities by presenting entertaining, vivid and thought-provoking descriptions of the vicissitudes of the therapeutic journey. Issues such as contracting, boundaries, confrontation, self-disclosure on the part of the therapist, dream interpretation, the influence of the consulting-room environment and conflicting belief systems are explored and challenged, providing the reader with a rich resource for their own thinking and discussion. In the light of today's political climate surrounding regulation of the psychological therapies, perhaps the stories might serve to illustrate the inappropriateness (and impossibility) of a one-size-fits-all, tick-box approach to working with people in distress.

I hope these stories will have particular interest for students nearing the end of their training and wishing to engage with the realities and the potential experiences of practising counselling and psychotherapy. To this end the stories may be used as course material to provide a springboard for reflection, critical thinking and discussion.

I hope also that they will appeal to experienced practitioners, who may recognize and resonate with the issues and dilemmas faced by the therapist (and perhaps be reassured by them). The stories also present the practitioner with the challenge of therapeutic conundrums outside their experience with which to engage critically. As material for the therapy reading groups that are currently proliferating (as part of Continuing Professional Development), I trust these stories will provide a wide range of themes and issues for discussion and debate. Equally, the stories may be read simply for pleasure and enjoyment, whether the reader is involved in the field of counselling and psychotherapy or not. The language does not discriminate against the layperson's understanding and enjoyment of the stories simply as stories.

My intention in writing these tales was to delve into to the heart of the therapeutic encounter – the meeting of two people in a room to form a relationship with the endeavour of experiencing and understanding what it is to be human and, in so doing, bringing about change, specifically in the client, but inevitably also in the therapist. Though the stories must have their thematic origins somewhere in my actual experience as a therapist, any similarity to real clients is entirely unintentional. I have deliberately chosen to keep all the stories and the characters who inhabit them fictional. This has allowed me the poetic licence to take the stories where I thought they should go – though, in some instances, they seemed to take themselves (often to places I would have preferred they hadn't) – to explore specific themes and to consider various issues in the restricted, and therefore concentrated, space of the short story. Interestingly, despite writing in the first person, by the time I had written three or four of these stories I realized that the person of the therapist is partly fictitious too. I began to see him in my mind's eye as a few years older, more formally dressed and somewhat stouter than me (though I am gaining on him in this latter respect). I suddenly found him wearing a suit (which I wear only for weddings and funerals). I can only imagine that this separation of the writer from the character occurred outside my awareness to allow me a freer rein with the therapist too.

In the final chapter, following the 10 stories, I consider some of the themes and issues raised by them – in particular, drawing attention to the key challenges and providing some theoretical considerations. Under each story title, I invite the reader, whether student or practitioner, to consider from their own theoretical perspective what their particular approach to these issues might be. I provide questions to assist these considerations and discussions. Where appropriate, I suggest further reading to explore these issues in more detail and refer to textbooks on specific theoretical and technical aspects in which the reader may be interested. These discussion points and questions will hopefully allow the 'lay' reader also a glimpse into the theoretical thinking of a therapist.

I hope you enjoy the stories simply as stories that focus on the overall experience of the nature and culture of counselling and psychotherapy. At the same time, I hope you find them useful as starting points for considering your own theoretical perspective and practice. So, as you read through each of them, I encourage you to identify how you as the therapist might have responded to these clients and their issues, how you might have conceptualized the work and what you would have done differently – and why.

The Carving

Like most psychotherapists, I work in a room intentionally neutral in its décor and furnishings to allow my clients and their therapeutic relationship with me to be as unencumbered by extraneous intrusion or distraction as is possible. Family photographs and personal memorabilia have no place here, but to distinguish the room from a prison cell or a medical clinic, it does have bookshelves (admittedly housing only psychotherapy books), comfortable sofas, low tables, even a bowl of dried gourds – all of which must give away something of my stylistic tastes and preferences and say something about me, though limited to the confines of the consulting room. Equally, my choice of clothes, shoes, even the boxes of tissues I provide or my appointments diary must evoke some associations for my clients that might usefully be explored at some point in our work. Unlike more classical, psychoanalytic therapists, I'm not attempting to be a 'blank screen' or a 'non person' but to provide a fairly neutral and mutual exploratory space, the room as background to our relationship and our work together.

Recently, however, a wood-carver friend of mine gave me one of his carvings that I had coveted for some time but couldn't afford to buy. He entitled this generous gift, 'Tree in Wood from Tree'. It's an old, elm chair-seat through which have been carved three circles, two side by side above a larger one. Inside of these, the trunk and branches of a miniature tree have been 'exposed'. I use this word purposely as the carver's skill and artistry lies in the fact that the wood is all of a piece and the delicate, intricate branches within the holes have all been painstakingly created solely by carving from the chair seat – no insertions, no glue, just the removal of wood. I fell in love with it on first viewing and immediately made an association to the process of therapy – the painstaking uncovering, the exploration, the clearing away – to rediscover the unadulterated self hidden in the life-adapted person we all become. The young tree exposed in the old wood symbolized, for me, the potential of that original, unspoilt self still to be found (and reclaimed) within the ageing, and also to be treasured, adult through the process of psychotherapy. Its place in my therapy room was inevitable. There was even a wall, shared by the ends of the adjacent sofas but peripheral to my and my clients' view, that had a space just waiting to be filled.

For several weeks after hanging, the wooden carving appeared to have only singular influence. As clients arrived for their sessions, *I* was acutely aware of the brown square on the wall, like a vague shadow on the periphery of my vision, but none of my clients seemed to notice it, let alone remark on it as I had assumed they might. Quite rightly, of course, they were involved with themselves, with their own issues. They were drawn into their inner life, their past and present and projected worlds. A piece of wood on a wall was not their focus. I tried not to make it mine but I must admit it took some weeks before I got accustomed to its presence and could lessen its visual distraction.

Olive was the first to be affected by it – but only indirectly. She didn't seem to notice the carving at all. Instead, as she came into the room, she looked at the bookshelves and remarked, 'Oh, you've brought your books in here. It feels much more like a study now.' (This from someone who had sat in this room on a weekly basis for three years and had often stared at the bookshelves for long periods of time.) I can only surmise that the carving had made a visual, if indistinct, impression on her and that this had registered in her mind as 'there's something different in this room'. Quite why she thought it was the books was not immediately clear to me but she sat down still looking at them in a rather perplexed and anxious way.

'Does the room being more like a study have a particular meaning for you?' I asked, remembering that her father had been a vicar and that she had spent her early childhood living in a large manse. She had not talked much about him in all the time we had worked together, despite my prompting. Her depressed and narcissistic mother had monopolized Olive's focus in therapy as much as in life.

'It reminds me ...,' she began, but halted with trembling lips. Breathing deeply, she looked away from the books and into my eyes. 'It reminds me of things ... things to do with my father. I feel your books have given me permission to talk about him now. He was a dear man but ... '

And so a new and important phase of our work began.

Jack, in his mid-seventies, my oldest client at that time, was the first to notice and remark upon the carving directly but his association was very unexpected.

'We had those when I was a child,' he remarked as he leant a little in the direction of the carving, squeezing his eyes to narrow slits the better to see.

'Did you Jack?' I asked, assuming he meant that the wooden seat was familiar to him from his childhood home. 'Where was that?'

'Oh, that would be in Leicester,' he replied after a moment's reflection. 'We kept them under the stairs.'

'Last week you referred to your mother's proclivity for "keeping things for best"' I said. 'Was that why the chairs were under the stairs?'

Jack looked puzzled. 'I don't understand.'

'The wooden chairs, like the seat on the wall?'

'Seat on the ....' He petered out, a look of bewilderment on his face.

'I'm sorry,' I said. 'I wonder if we're talking at cross-purposes. I was assuming the wooden seat reminded you of chairs in your childhood home.'

'Chairs?' queried Jack. 'Who said anything about chairs? I'm talking about gas masks, you know, during the war?'

'I see,' I dissembled, not seeing at all. I glanced to the side to see what I was missing but saw only the carving, the tree within the wooden seat. 'Is that what the carving reminds you of?'

'Isn't that what it's meant to be?' he asked somewhat incredulously, an incredulity that was mutual in that moment (after all, why would I have a gas mask on the wall?). There was only one way to solve this puzzle.

'Can I come and sit next to you?' I asked on impulse, wanting to see what he was seeing. He readily agreed and I moved to sit at his side and looked directly at the carving. The winter sun was at such an angle that from Jack's position the intricacies of the tree, its trunk and branches, were in shadow and unclear. The three holes gaped dark and starkly within the seat. I could see clearly the two round eyes of the goggles above the larger mouthpiece where the canister of charcoal would have been. Though obvious now, it would never have occurred to me to see a gas mask unprompted. It was now hard not to see it.

Jack gently reached across and patted my hand, 'Before your time, young man,' he chuckled.

'Only just,' I protested. 'But it's a very big "just" isn't it? Your wartime childhood must have been very different from mine.'

'I'll tell you about it. You probably need to know,' said Jack.

I couldn't tell if he meant for my own benefit as a comparatively lucky post-war baby or for my professional knowledge in order to help him. Either way, I looked forward to hearing of his experiences, including what it must have been like in those threatening times to have gas masks hanging ready under the stairs. However, I realize now, I never did discover why he thought I might decorate my wall with a gas mask, carving or not.

As it happened, the mask theme continued when I was working with Deborah, a young and successful actor now training as a psychotherapist who came to therapy as part of her training. She was not, like some students I've worked with, simply clocking up the required hours. She was a dedicated client, keen to explore and examine her life, eager to bring into practice the theoretical concepts she was learning about and apply them to herself. In the session just after Jack's, it was she who introduced Winnicott's idea of the 'True' and 'False' self as it made a lot of sense to her in relation to her acting career. She felt her success on the stage was due to her effortless ability to present a false persona so convincingly. When acting a part, she *was* that person. She 'lost' herself in the character of another. It was a very creative way to employ a false self.

I appreciated her application of the theory and I admired her willingness to analyse herself in this way but I felt she was missing something by applying the concept solely to her career. I suggested this was perhaps not a phenomenon restricted to the stage. More challengingly, I told her that I sometimes felt she was not there, that the persona I saw – albeit a delightful, laughing and bubbly young woman – was hiding her real self away, protecting her, keeping her safe. I clearly touched upon something true for her as her eyes filled and tears rolled down her cheeks.

'You're right, I don't feel real when I'm off the stage. In fact, I sometimes feel more real when I'm acting a part,' she sobbed. 'I sometimes feel I can't take it off.'

'Take it off?' I enquired.

'The mask,' she answered. 'It's like your laughing mask is welded to my face.'

Sensitized by Jack's gas mask, I immediately knew she meant the carving. Indeed, this time I didn't need to look to know what Deborah meant by the 'laughing mask'. Those three holes – the wide, circular eyes and the gaping mouth – were clearly the apertures of a dramatic mask, a gaping of fixed hilarity, a mask to hide the tears. I suggested she turn and face the carving directly and to see what came to her mind.

As she did so, she said unprompted, 'Hello sunshine' and burst into tears again.

I waited. Eventually she glanced across at me. 'It's what my dad called me … still calls me …'

'Sunshine,' I repeated.

'… but it's not real … I can't be his sunshine all the time.' She sobbed again. 'I shouldn't have to do that to be special.'

She faced the mask again and stared at it in silence for quite some time.

'Is there something else you want to say?' I asked eventually.

'Thank you,' she said unexpectedly.

'Thank you for …?' I prompted.

'Thank you for getting me through as best you could.' She sighed as she addressed the mask. 'I gained a lot through you. I lost a lot too. Maybe I need to find what I gave up on all those years ago. Maybe then I can be more real.'

For many of my clients the carving seemed to have no impact and figured not at all in our work together (at least consciously). For others it became a focal point for a while and for some a reference point to be returned to every now and again. I was amazed at the variety and ingenuity of human perception and interpretation. It reminded me of a truism from the Talmud that says, 'We do not see things as they are. We see things as we are'.

For Serena the holes were circular windows screened by the branches of a shrub: the garden den in which she hid, frightened and alone, to avoid the savage fights between her parents indoors, terrified of what she might find on her return. For Alice, the intricate, interlocking branches reminded her of the lace her grandmother would crochet as she sat by the fire and told fascinating stories of the past, while for Jon the carving more concretely evoked memories of his father and the smell of saw-dust and wood shavings, a sweaty masculinity that entered the house in the evenings on his father's return and which he realized had been his saving grace within the cloyingly feminine environment of his mother and five sisters.

The most recent, and most unusual perceptions of the carving have come from one of my younger clients, Brian, a wiry, bespectacled 18-year-old with strabismus in his left eye which he says doesn't bother him (his glasses correct the tendency of his eye to turn outwards) but which sometimes makes him look as if he's daydreaming. Though now clean for a year, Brian regularly smoked skunk from an early age and, according to the referring psychiatrist, may be severely damaged by his frequent and continuous use of the drug. Suffering from episodes of paranoia and confusion, Brian fears so too. But most of the time, and always with me, he's a presentable, intelligent and likeable young man indistinguishable from many a late-teenager struggling with the demands of growing up, finding a career, a girlfriend and a meaning to life. And these have been the recurring themes of our work together over the past few months though more in the realms of discussion than action. The problem is that what he calls his 'bonkers episodes' interfere with each of these, at least, his fear of the occurrence of these episodes does. He's reluctant to commit to anything that might expose him as 'bonkers' despite the fact that the episodes occur infrequently. Unfortunately, this means he isolates himself in his bedroom at home, watching daytime TV, surfing the Internet, or sleeping a great deal and avoiding taking action in any of the areas in which he would otherwise be more actively engaged. He hasn't yet applied to university to follow his former enthusiasm for the Arts in general, and Modern English Literature in particular. Likewise, his reticence to socialize prevents the possibility of meeting any young people for friendships let alone deeper relationships. He makes do with fantasies of female pop stars and Internet 'chats' with young women. He claims to meet hundreds of girlfriends on Facebook but I challenge his use of the words 'meet' and 'girlfriends' when all he's doing is looking at photographs (sometimes not even that) and typing words into the ether. He doesn't like me to confront his fantasy life but I sometimes point out that in some ways it's just as out of touch with reality as his so-called 'bonkers episodes'. Not surprisingly, finding meaning in life from the confines of his bedroom, cut off from others (even his parents seem to leave him to himself in the belief he's going to 'snap out of it' spontaneously) and with nothing to excite or engage him is almost a non-starter. He has, however, following a visit from the local vicar at his parents' request, started to believe in a god – unfortunately, an Old Testament one who is watching in judgment and about to administer some dreadful punishment at any moment. This doesn't help his paranoid thinking at all so

I challenge his belief quite strongly: it's always struck me as odd that approaches to psychotherapy that specifically encourage the confrontation of irrational beliefs ignore the most glaring of them all. I've suggested we call his god 'Yahweh' just to put him in some sort of context, namely the superstitious belief of a primitive tribe a few thousand years ago in a Middle Eastern desert.

Never having witnessed Brian in the grip of a 'bonkers episode', I've yet to be fully convinced of the psychiatrist's diagnosis of 'cannabis psychosis'. I can see that he is generally unmotivated, and at times extremely apathetic (like most teenagers) but the attendant criteria of memory loss, auditory and visual illusions or hallucinations are not present (or reported on). The one thing he does report is his occasional paranoid thinking that god or others are watching him though, again, this has not occurred in our sessions. Brian only reports on his paranoia outside the sessions, and even then I'm not convinced he really believes in thunderbolts from heaven except by way of a metaphorical punishment: 'Surely something bad will happen if I stay in bed all morning'. Even his belief that others may think he's rather strange and, therefore, want to persecute him seems to me to have become a cultivated avoidance-technique for isolating himself, almost certainly not psychotic. Basically, I think the calming, slightly euphoric effect of dope held off an underlying depression for years and, without it, he's experiencing the reality of his unhappiness.

But, a few sessions ago, I started to question my more benign diagnosis. Brian began expressing some strange thoughts, out of the blue, totally unconnected to any topic we had been discussing. It was almost as if a switch had been thrown in his brain. On one such occasion we were exploring ways in which he might safely structure some gradual steps towards venturing out more socially into the world. I counted his visits to me as part of the venturing out that he had already achieved – and could build upon – given that he had to travel quite a way by bus in the company of others, albeit without interacting with them. I asked whether he might practise simply saying 'Hello' to a fellow passenger each trip, at which point the brain switch seemed to be thrown. He removed his glasses and his eyes took on the daydreaming quality I had noticed before as his eyes lost their focus.

'He's very cute,' he said. 'I like the way he smiles.'

'Someone cute on the bus smiles at you?' I enquired, noticing the gender and already racing ahead with the thought that Brian was about to reveal that he was gay. It could explain so much about his isolating himself. In a still homophobic society (culturally if not legislatively) and with parents who probably have strong religious views on the subject of homosexuality (perhaps thunderbolts, hell and damnation included), it would make so much sense of his struggles with fitting in and his paranoid thinking that others might be judging him. But I was stopped in my over-zealous tracks.

'No,' he continued emphatically. 'The frog. I like the way the frog smiles.'

I managed to retain my composure as I explored further with, 'A frog on the bus?'

'No, there,' he laughed, nodding in my direction. 'Can't you see it?' There was almost a teasing note in his voice which seemed unusually enlivened.

'Do you mean me?' I ventured in response to the inferred joke.

'No, you're not a frog are you?' he replied, while I wondered if I was picking up his paranoid habits. Thinking he might be looking behind me, I turned to the windowsills on either side of my sofa. I also looked out of the windows wondering if maybe some intrepid frog had scaled up the outside wall to the first floor.

'He looks a bit like Kermit,' stated Brian in a matter-of-fact manner while I searched in vain for the elusive frog.

At a loss, I decided to follow the Muppet connection. 'Is that something you watch on television?'

'Oh yes,' he affirmed. 'I know it's a bit naff but daytime TV is altogether pretty crap and some of it's quite funny. Not just for young kids really.'

'And what does Kermit mean to you?' I asked.

'Nothing really,' he answered looking rather bored at my attempt to psychologize a Muppet. 'He's just a frog. But a frog with a nice smile. I like that.'

I realized the end of the session was upon us so I quickly asked, 'And were you thinking about a smiling frog like Kermit just now in your mind's eye.'

'No,' said Brian, putting on his spectacles. 'I could see him.'

Despite my attempts in the following session to explore the frog further in order to better ascertain it's meaning as well as the possibility of a visual hallucination, Brian was having none of it preferring instead to consider the stupidity of the public vote on *X Factor*. I gave up on frogs and tried to build on the theme of judgment in relation to his thoughts of others being critical of him. I pointed out the incongruence between the credence he gave the imagined judgement of *his* 'public', and the stupidity he allotted to *X Factor* viewers. I might as well have been discussing knitting patterns with Kermit for the amount of insight this brought into fruition. It was not a productive session. Nor was the next one. Towards the end of the following session, the futility of trying to engage Brian in exploring anything meaningful in his interminable ramblings sank in as I sank lower on the sofa. I was totally bored (and probably angry) and more to keep myself awake than anything else, I returned to our previous focus of devising a structured, step-by-step programme for getting him out of the house and into the company of others. I mentioned again the possibility of saying hello to passengers on the bus. Brian chose to take out a grey, crumpled handkerchief and clean his glasses.

'That's my brain, that is,' he stated, breathing onto and polishing the lenses. 'Just like that.'

I struggled to see the connection. 'Your glasses are like your brain? As you polish the lenses you see some link to your brain?'

'No,' he said. 'Not my glasses. All those mixed-up wires ... that's my brain ... All criss-crossed.'

I had the impression he was looking where he had previously seen the frog, but as with the amphibian I could see nothing resembling a brain.

These sudden 'visions' occurred sporadically over the next few sessions. Frogs, brains, faces, tunnels, snakes would be remarked upon – with a smile or a laugh – a propos of nothing of which we were talking. Interpretation (yes, the obvious in the case of the tunnels and snakes) got us nowhere and I was beginning to concur with the psychiatrist – perhaps, he was hallucinating after all. And if so, I began to wonder just how much help I could really be to him faced with what might be organic rather than psychological damage. The worst session of all was last week. Not only did Kermit reappear (to him, if not to me) but a collection of squares and circles, caves and caverns, pits and stairways, even the face of god. For a moment I believed I was witnessing one of his 'bonkers episodes', perhaps a manifestation of his cannabis psychosis.

Sitting with him, however, I was still not convinced. There was something about his joking that left me feeling uncomfortable; not as one might in the presence of madness, more in the presence of manipulation. I wanted to detach myself from what I suspected was some sort of game. I allowed myself to break present contact with him and wander back in my mind over our times together. I looked for a pattern. I looked for triggers. I discovered they had been staring me in the face. It was time for a gentle show-down.

'I notice you don't have your glasses on today,' I observed nonchalantly.

'No,' he replied. 'They're broken.'

'Is that difficult for you?' I asked. 'I mean, is it difficult for you to focus straight ahead?'

'Might be,' he said shifting uneasily on the sofa.

'You're not looking at me right now are you?' I suggested, feeling my way into my theory.

'I can see you well enough,' he said, with a belligerent edge to his tone of voice.

'But only vaguely,' I suggested. 'I think your left eye has drifted; it's seeing more to your left than straight ahead. You're looking more at the carving than at me.'

'Maybe,' he pouted sulkily.

I stood and walked to the carving. Leaning closer to it, I traced a finger over various points of the chair seat, outlining the shapes and indentations as I named them.

'So here is Kermit – here's his mouth where the middle strut of the chair back would have been, and his two eyes are here where the staves have left holes. Here are the criss-crossed wires of the brain – the interweaving branches of the tree. This is the stairway. Here is the snake. Here is the cave. And here even the face of god, I think.'

Brian was looking sheepish. Though he said nothing, I could see that I had unearthed the origins of his visual 'hallucinations'.

'I'm relieved,' I said. 'For a moment I thought you were going totally bonkers.'

'Maybe I am,' protested Brian.

'No,' I asserted. 'I think you're simply scared.'

'What's to be scared of?' he asked, attempting to sound confident. 'I'm not scared.'

'I think you're scared of lots of things,' I persisted. 'I think you're scared of the world, especially the people in it.'

For a moment I thought he was getting up to leave the room but he was, in fact, simply rising to gain access to something in his pocket. He took out his glasses and put them on. I refrained from commenting on their miraculous repair. I simply waited for him to speak.

'I like the carving,' he said. 'I like seeing so many things in it.'

'Yes,' I said softly. 'I believe you do. I like that you've unveiled so much in the chair seat. It's wonderful, your imagination … it can open a world of possibilities. Paradoxically, it can also be very restricting. It can act as a deflection from reality.'

'Yes?' he queried and I told him how I'd worked out the triggers and the pattern: how each time I'd suggested some means of connecting with people in the outside world, he'd removed his glasses and, as a result of his strabismus and his wandering left eye, focused on the carving, losing himself (and me) in his imaginings. In response, he cried, more from the unburdening, I think, than sadness at being discovered.

'Let's use it more creatively,' I suggested. 'Let's use the carving more as a deliberation than a deflection. We can come back to socializing at some future point. I think I rushed you. Let's play with what we can find in that simple wooden seat.'

'OK,' agreed Brian with an audible sigh of relief. Then he paused a while before looking me straight in the eye and asking, 'I'm not bonkers am I?'

'No more than any of us,' I replied honestly.

In the quiet of the evening after a working day, often with the sun reaching soft and low into the room, I sometimes lie along the sofa used by my clients and contemplate the carving and the phantasmagoria it engenders. I can see what each of my clients have seen in it and the meaning they have made out of it. I can see the fantastic images they have carved, not with chisels, but with their creative imagination, and I marvel at the mind's ingenuity. I sometimes see my own strange images and ponder on just why they have occurred to me (why that, why now?), but mostly I see the 'tree in wood from tree' that first attracted me – and in that I sense my younger self. I feel him as part of me, ever youthful, ever energetic, ever influential, inside my tired and ageing body.

Subterranean

Imagine the timidity of a mouse. Now multiply it by ten and you'll have some idea of Daniel. Sitting opposite me in his worn-shiny, grey suit, it was not hard to add a few whiskers; the similitude was completed by the occasional tiny squeak of a voice from his pursed, twitching lips.

Our weekly sessions in my consulting room just off the Holloway Road were not at the best time of day – at least, not for me. I usually felt enervated after a morning's work and a good lunch but I had convinced myself that my lowered energy in that first session of the afternoon well suited Daniel. I considered I was more able to match his slow pace, his quiet demeanour and his need of a gentle ear.

We had worked together in my London practice for just over a year since the spring of 2004 trying to understand, and attempting to overcome, his compliant and over-adapted way of being in the world. It was not *that* hard to understand. If you put a sadistic, military man together with a shy, retiring woman who then produce between them one son of a rather sickly constitution, the end result of a 'mouse' is not altogether surprising. The task of changing the result, as now manifested in this 40-year-old man, was not so easy.

When he had visited his widowed mother in Highbury, our sessions always began with minute details of his mother's ailments and what they had eaten for lunch before he left to see me. Every other session began with a story of his journey across London: his walk from his attic bed-sit (so suitable for a mouse that I sometimes imagined it full of hay and torn newspaper bedding) to the South Kensington tube, the unpredictability of the Piccadilly Line, the delays, the queues, the weather on emerging at Holloway Road, his uneventful walk to my house — and the mild, controlled pleasure he expressed that despite the vicissitudes of London Transport, he'd arrived exactly on time, again.

'I wonder how you imagine I might feel were you to be late for a session,' I once enquired.

Daniel raised his eyes from the spot on the carpet that usually gripped his attention and looked at me.

'Oh, I would never be late,' he said, almost inaudibly.

'No, but imagine if you were,' I persisted. 'How do you think I might feel?'

'If I were late, which I wouldn't be really, I'd phone you on my mobile.'

I was tempted to go down the 'yes, but what if' route of forgotten mobiles, vandalized telephone boxes, power cuts, all usual manner of communications being impossible but I could sense this was not the way to go. I was feeling irritated. We were playing 'cat and mouse' and I knew that more such qualifications might have me pouncing, maybe 'devouring' him, diminishing him even more, as his father had done in the past.

I took a breath and calmed myself. I pondered on his father's physically and psychologically sadistic approach to parenting. I thought too of Daniel as a child at the receiving end of such cruelty and of the rage he must be containing still from those early days. If only he could get to that … I felt so far it was *I* who was feeling all the anger.

'I guess you were never late for your father either,' I gently suggested.

Daniel sat in silence, his eyes back to the carpet. But I surmised a change of colour in that grey, shrunken face. Perhaps, there was a feeling going on somewhere as he recalled times with his father.

'No,' he whispered eventually. 'I was never late.'

Over the year, Daniel's weekly accounts of his journey to each session continued. Trying to make some sense of this and utilize it to some purpose, I encouraged him to explore the symbolism of his weekly trek across the metropolis, likening the underground to submerged unconscious processes, to emotions surging deep beneath the surface, to existential choices (though he always took the Piccadilly Line), even to mouse-holes in which to hide anonymously amongst the other rodents of the daily rat-race (yes, we'd shared the 'timid mouse' analogy early on; it was unavoidable; as was the corollary of my cat-like presence in the room), and, of course, to his equally winding, undulating journey in his psychotherapy with me.

Did it help? I have to honestly admit, I don't know, but at the very least it got us communicating. He was sharing something of himself, however vague and sparse. That was not something he did in the outside world where, ensconced in the bowels of the British Museum (another subterranean mouse-hole) labelling ancient artefacts (more symbolism to be explored) or reading archaeology books in the evenings in his attic-nest, he lived an isolated life. Perhaps then, in the comparative safety of his 50 minutes with me, this psychological archaeology had its place. It provided a catalyst for relating to another human being.

But the past and his weekly journey were not the only topics he brought to the sessions. Though they were few and far between, Daniel would recount some incident that had occurred during the week. Of course, when I say 'recount', I mean 'slowly unfold'. Haltingly and often excruciatingly painstakingly, he would describe some happening he had witnessed or been party to. It was at moments like this that I felt my most feline, wanting to pounce on the prey, play with it, get my teeth into it. I literally bit my tongue at times, afraid I would scare the little mouse back into his hole if I spoke too soon.

'And then the manager came down ...' Daniel went on recently, continuing a seemingly inconsequential story that had now taken us into the second half of the session. He paused again as he groped for exactly the right words. I noticed his fingers drumming on his knee, an agitation I had drawn attention to in the past to no avail.

'… he asked me to take some files to his office …'. Another pause. 'That's not my job …'. His drumming quickened. 'That's not what I'm employed to do …'.

I could see he was more agitated now. The drumming increased and beneath the grey pallor of his face, I could detect a rising flush. Though his voice remained at its usual quiet pitch, there was something in it that was different, something about his more pronounced enunciation through those pursed lips that altered its timbre. I knew he was feeling angry.

In the minutes that ticked by, I found myself hoping to hear that he'd got up from his seat, faced the manager, told him in no uncertain terms that he was busy with the work he was meant to be doing and would not deliver the files to his office. This was, of course, a fantastic expectation. It was my aspiration for him – I believe the therapist sometimes needs to hold the hope the client is unable to dream of. One day, perhaps, I would hear such a denouement. It would not be today.

'… I took the files to his office,' Daniel went on, raising his eyes cursorily, checking, perhaps, to see a hint of disappointment in my face, 'but only later … only after I'd finished what I was doing.'

Compared to my so-in-the-distant-future hope, this fell far short but for Daniel this was an enormous step and one I wished to affirm.

'So you didn't jump to his orders as you might have done in the past,' I observed. 'You didn't drop everything to obey him.'

'No,' he agreed (with was that a faint smile?).

'You were angry at being asked to take the files,' I suggested rather riskily (the anger word being one I used infrequently).

I pushed it further. 'In your way, you expressed your anger.'

Perhaps this was too much. Perhaps I had pounced too soon. It was one thing for Daniel to have told me he had passively resisted rushing to fulfil a demand, quite another for me to suggest this might have been anger. Daniel sat in silence, his eyes drawn back to the security of the spot on the carpet. Would he passively resist my demand too? Could I dare suggest that his slow, faltering stories were indeed another expression of his anger, however passive the mode? No, not yet, this would have been far too big a leap and maybe I had leapt too far already. I was relieved when he tentatively concurred.

'Yes, in a way,' he whispered. 'I certainly kept him waiting.'

'Yes, you kept him waiting. Not something you would have done with your father,' I observed yet again, wanting to emphasize the enormity of this development in his behaviour.

'No,' he replied almost immediately. 'I would not keep my father waiting.'

I was certain I noticed a change in his posture, a slight unfolding of his shoulders, a somewhat surer step as he left at the end of the session.

Behaving in a passively aggressive way is not something I would normally encourage. There are some clients whose whole modus operandi is based upon such an angry resistance to the demands of life and who come into therapy puzzled as to why they have few friends and struggle with intimacy. They have no idea just how irritating their indirect attacks can be, how their procrastination comes across to others as a lack of commitment, their 'forgetfulness' as indifference and their lateness as an insult. But for Daniel this was progress. Not to jump to the demands of others was a watershed. At least, I hoped it was. In this one incident, the mouse had stood his ground, albeit for just a few minutes. Because of it, I could see more clearly the possibility of Daniel unearthing his pent-up rage and, eventually, transforming it to healthy assertion.

Over the next few weeks I looked for signs that might show further development in Daniel's mild resistance. There were some. To anyone else they might have seemed totally insignificant. To me they indicated a healthy psychological process taking place.

He had in the past mentioned the poor lighting in the basement room in which he worked at the museum. I had encouraged him to complain, assuring him there must be Health and Safety Regulations which specified a level of light conducive to his work. Daniel had found this suggestion too difficult to even contemplate and continued to work in these most unsatisfactory circumstances. But now, having discovered a means of making some impact on his surroundings, he utilized it rather cleverly. Usually meticulous in his labelling of the artefacts, Daniel began to make mistakes: an un-dotted 'i' here, a somewhat irregular 'w' there, even a slight smudge of the copperplate curlicue of a capital 'C'. This, of course, went against the whole grain of his conditioning. However, overcoming his internal voices, his former precision was sacrificed for The Cause. Without comment from the management, the mistakes were returned to him for rewriting. Without explanation, the lighting level was raised.

Other victories of this kind ensued. Of course, they were minor victories in a world where more head-on assertion would one day be needed if Daniel were to begin to relate to other human beings in any meaningful way. He would need to show his feelings more directly. But, for now, I felt pleased at the way things were going. We continued our sessions in the slow, ponderous fashion that Daniel had required (perhaps, dictated?) from the start.

There was one thing that concerned me as time went on: I was getting increasingly tired during Daniel's early afternoon session. The combination of his faltering, over-detailed stories and my worsening post-lunch drop in energy found me, at times, almost nodding off in my chair. I could no longer convince myself that this was a 'good thing' for Daniel. It was one thing to match his pace, quite another to fall behind it. But a solution came fortuitously when a client with whom I had worked successfully for several years decided to end her therapy at the end of June. This meant a vacant session on Thursday mornings, Daniel's usual day of the week for his therapy with me. I had a month to forewarn him of this change of time and work through any feelings, however vague, he might have in response.

When I first put it to him, the idea was greeted with predictable acquiescence. He quietly assured me that 9.15 on a Thursday morning would be fine. It would be no problem at all. Thursday was his regular day off work so the timing was irrelevant. Yes, he was happy to move to the new time in the first week in July. No, it was not too early for him to travel across town.

I wondered whether, if he asked, I would disclose the reason for the rescheduling but, rather true to form, he requested no such information. I raised the change of time in the following few sessions to the same accepting response. It was only in the final session at our traditional time that I could see he was not really happy with the change. His drumming fingers belied his previous reassuring words.

'I notice you're drumming your fingers,' I interjected into a silence. 'And I wonder what they might be saying to you – and to me.'

'I don't know,' he replied after a time, sounding slightly irritated.

I couldn't let this pass without further comment. 'I guess they may be saying, "I don't like this change".'

His mouth was twitching but he said nothing.

I pressed on. 'I know you assure me that it's not an inconvenience. Nonetheless, it is something of an imposition. You might even see it as a demand.'

His fingers stopped drumming. I suspected he was controlling them, willing them not to betray him. He sat hunched into himself. Totally still now. Totally silent.

'It would be very understandable if you felt irritated by my changing the time,' I persisted, feeling certain this was an opportunity not to be missed. Would he risk it? Would he take my permission to share his irritation, however mildly expressed? Could he see that this was a chance to stand up to his 'father' and react to his demands? Could he for once admit to being impacted by my actions? He sat forward in his chair. I waited.

'I don't ...' he began, but stopped. It was painful to watch the contortions on his face, the effort of will to make himself speak. He was stuttering now. Daniel was a mumbler but not a stutterer. I could tell he was feeling something but I could only sit and wait.

'I don't ...' he continued. 'I ... I can't ... I can't get to it.'

'But it's there,' I affirmed softly.

'I think so,' he replied in a whisper.

Sometimes sessions end too soon. But I felt this was a good moment, dictated by the clock, to be ending. Daniel looked exhausted by his efforts. I smiled fondly at him and I reminded him of the time for the next session. He mumbled his 'goodbye' with a quick glance into my eyes.

The following Thursday I was keen to see if we could continue what seemed to me to be the beginning of a breakthrough for Daniel. I was also curious to observe how the change of timing (and my more alert morning energy) might influence the sessions. As always, I sat in my chair a few minutes before the session to ponder as I awaited Daniel's arrival. At 9.15 I listened for the sound of the front door and Daniel's light footsteps along the hall. But none came. I imagined that the change of timing would have added considerably to his journey. After all, the rush hour would still be in full sway. But still, it was odd. Daniel was the sort of person to have made allowances for this. Everything would have been taken into account. He prided himself on his punctuality.

I sat waiting for a few minutes before going to check I had unlocked the front door. I was almost certain I had and, in any case, there was a bell for such situations, though I preferred my clients to let themselves in and for me be waiting for them in my consulting room. Sure enough, the door was not locked.

I returned to my room. I felt concerned but found myself wondering if Daniel's journey at a different time would bring forth a shift in the familiar stories: a more workaday crowd, perhaps a greater sense of connection, of purpose, bustling along in the morning traffic. I looked forward to exploring the new symbolism that his real and metaphorical, subterranean journey might evoke.

By 9.30 I was worried. I decided to phone his mobile. Perhaps an unusual thing to do but I wanted Daniel to know I was concerned, that I was holding him in mind. And, mindful of his words 'I would not keep my father waiting', I wanted him to know that I was waiting with concern, not anger. As it was, I could not reach him by mobile. It appeared there was some service fault and the phone merely beeped at me.

He did not turn up. At the end of the 50 minutes I took my usual stroll in the garden to clear my mind for my next client. I saw three that morning but, though my concentration was good enough, I was not fully engaged. My thoughts kept wandering to Daniel.

In retrospect, it was odd that none of my clients had mentioned the events that had occurred earlier that morning. Perhaps, like me, they had not heard. It was only when I switched on the 1 o'clock news that I learnt of the terrorist attacks. At first, it seemed unreal, more like some fictional drama. I couldn't immediately take in the details. The newsreader spoke of bombs, explosions, casualties in the underground. A police commissioner reported 150 people injured and 'a number' of fatalities. The detail I heard most clearly was that at 8.56am a device had exploded on a train between King's Cross and Russell Square. This was Daniel's route – of which I knew vicariously every twist and turn, every advertisement, every click of the rails.

My first instinctive reaction was to call him again despite the previous failed attempt. My legs were weak as I stumbled to the phone and my hands were trembling as I dialled. As before, the line was dead. I admitted to my consciousness, for the first time since the news, that maybe he was too. I went into my consulting room, sat in my chair and shook uncontrollably. The enormity of my responsibility had hit me. No amount of rationalizations could comfort me. It was as if I had pushed Daniel into the lions' den: a Daniel not as equipped as his biblical counterpart, with lions who were not so easily tamed. I could not rid my mind of Daniel, harmless and innocent, travelling in that subterranean time bomb: the time dictated by me. I sat and felt wretched.

One would have thought my circadian rhythm would have been over-ridden by the extremity of the circumstances, though I suppose my tiredness may also have been due to the draining of my emotional as well as physical resources as I sat for some time berating myself for my decision. Whatever had caused my drop in energy, I realized I had fallen asleep when I woke with a start, aware that someone was in the room. The clock read 2pm.

He sat there opposite me. To begin with, I wasn't sure if he really sat there or whether I had conjured him up in my disturbed, dozing dreams.

'Daniel?' I said tentatively. 'Are you OK?'

'Yes,' he replied, not knowing just how welcome that quiet, squeaky voice was to my ears.

I smiled. 'I am so pleased you are here.'

He looked slightly uncomfortable as he asked, 'You're not angry?'

'Angry?' I said and added instantly. 'No, my dear Daniel, far from it. I'm delighted to see you.'

He groped for the words.

'You were asleep,' he said after a while. 'It's the wrong time. I just didn't want to come in the morning.'

'Oh,' I said, trying to get my head around what was happening, trying to become a therapist again.

With his usual faltering, he slowly continued, 'I intended to come … I stayed at my mother's last night to avoid the rush hour. But I knew I didn't like the change … so I didn't come.'

'So you're here now at your regular time,' I said. 'Daniel, that's absolutely fine by me.'

He smiled. I sat and smiled back and felt for the first time a real contact between us. He neither twitched nor drummed his fingers but sat relaxed as we held each other's gaze. I let the moment linger, savouring it like a taste of something deliciously sweet.

When eventually his eyes left mine, I asked, 'Do you know what's happened today?'

Without hesitation, he replied, 'Yes, in my way, I've shown you my anger.'

This was not what I had meant at all by my question but his answer was a joy. While others were expressing their anger so aggressively, so destructively, so very indiscriminately, I was thankful that Daniel, no longer the mouse, had staged his own gentle revolution.

Holding Boundaries

When Helen announced that she'd not only met a man at a salsa class the previous week but also arranged to meet him again, I must admit to a certain smug satisfaction. It would have been unthinkable for her to make such an announcement three years ago when she first came to see me and I felt delighted that our work together had reached this point of … well, if not fruition, at least budding. Whatever might happen next with this man, it was an enormous step for Helen to have got this far. Mind you, I have to concede that her previous therapy with my colleague, Tessa, had laid the vital foundations, and more. Without their work together, Helen would not have had the courage to leave her female therapist and risk therapy with a man.

Helen, now in her late thirties, had been wary of men for most of her life and understandably so. Her alcoholic father had abandoned her when she was two years old and her step-father, also an alcoholic, had not only been violent to her ineffectual mother but sexually abusive and sadistically cruel to Helen throughout her childhood and teenage years. Not surprisingly, throughout most of her adult life Helen had avoided men at all cost. To her, they (we) were all abusers. For many years, she worked in a women's refuge, lived in a women's collective and sought only women's company wherever possible. Her life might have continued this way quite satisfactorily but for two things. Firstly, she longed for an intimate and sexual relationship. Secondly, she was not sexually attracted to women. How much easier if she had been – but her experiments with lesbian partners had just not worked. It seemed to her she had two choices: to be alone and celibate for the rest of her life or, as she put it, 'sleep with the enemy', which was also very much how she saw coming into therapy with me.

And here we were, three years on, after many stormy times locked in battle or in a stand-off or just simply locked, going nowhere, hating each other from our respective sides of the gender line. Here we were, having survived, having discovered how to love and respect each other across that constructed line, feeling optimistic that Helen's longing for a relationship with a man could and would be fulfilled. The session, my first of a very busy day, ended with a happily tearful Helen dancing a few salsa steps by the door before leaving. It seemed to me to be a spontaneous embodiment of her delight in her achievement – spontaneity in the presence of a man being, perhaps, the greatest achievement of all – a sign of her past traumas having been worked through, a sign of the presence of trust.

It was a long day. By the time my last session was half-way through I was exhausted. Truth to tell, I was always exhausted when working with Lee. Occasionally, we would meet earlier in the day, but it made little odds. There was just something relentlessly draining about him and I had not yet got the measure of how to regulate my energy to prevent heavy waves of tiredness washing over me. To put it bluntly, he was 'wired' like a whippet in a cage and the more excited and talkative he became, the more my energy flagged. I wondered if there was some correlation between our energies – switch his up and mine would go down, switch mine up … but, no, it didn't work that way round. Switch mine up and his would increase proportionally. Six months in and I was already considering an onward referral, probably to someone younger.

Lee was in his early twenties but years of hard drugs and living by his adrenalin-fuelled wits had added at least a decade to his thin, hollow-cheeked, angular looks. He'd had a tough life on the streets and would be there still had it not been for his arrest and his eventual successful rehabilitation while serving his sentence for grievous bodily harm inflicted on a female traffic warden. A charity linked to the Young Offenders scheme now paid for him to see me for what they termed 'behavioural difficulties stemming from inadequate parenting' and which Lee referred to as 'Losing it because I was fucked up by scumbag shit-heads'. I think Larkin would have agreed with him – as did I, for that matter. But I have to confess, though I felt sorry for Lee and his disadvantaged start in life, I didn't warm to him or find much empathy within myself to provide the mirroring he so sadly lacked. Apart from being exhausted by his nervous energy, I found his storytelling, his confabulation (a remnant from his former alcoholism if not a life-long survival strategy), just downright tedious and irritating. How does one mirror a mirage? I wanted to fall asleep. He was off on one again …

'So I told George that I couldn't do a late shift at the depot on Monday 'cos I was meeting my social worker at the Boston at eight 'cos she wanted to talk about my trip to Goa in the summer. Well, he was livid but he's got no right to even ask me … .' He gabbled on.

'Lee …' I repeated his name several times before he stopped. Already I was wondering if it was worth the effort. But, no, I had to challenge this nonsense before it became fixed in his mind as a truth, if it hadn't become one already. 'Lee, I think your manager has every right to ask you to do a late shift. And you have every right to say "No" to a late shift. But you don't have to invent a whole story as an excuse. You can just say "No, thanks" and ...'

'Are you calling me a liar?' put in Lee, his limbs twitching as if an electric current ran through them, his face seeming to exude sparks. ''Cos if you are, I don't like that. I don't come here to be told that. That's totally out of order …'

'I'm saying you didn't have to invent a story,' I continued, braving his further wrath. 'To begin with, your social worker is a man. He doesn't work in the evenings. The Boston closes at 7 o'clock. And your summer holiday is to Gosport, not Goa.'

'So?' said Lee. I felt any last remaining energy drain away.

By the time the next Wednesday came along, I was looking forward to starting the day with Helen and hearing how her date had gone. I found myself hoping it had gone well and that there would be some continuing of their meeting if only as a practice run on the way to developing a more intimate relationship with a man. She had already taken employment in a mixed office and moved out of the women's collective into a shared house with two men and three women. These first steps to normalizing the male species had proved successful. Her joining a salsa class had been a further development, and one she enjoyed greatly (her few steps at the end of last week's session indicated quite a natural talent for Latin dancing), but a one-to-one meeting with a man, away from the safety of a mixed crowd, away from our sessions where she felt protected and held by the boundaries of our professional relationship, was an enormous leap.

She arrived unusually late and seemed flustered and anxious. I made an observation to this effect, wondering if things had gone badly after all. 'No, not at all,' Helen panted, suggesting she had run here to avoid arriving even later. She held up her hand as if for me to let her catch her breath before further talk. Eventually she added, 'I'm sorry. I was up rather late last night and didn't hear the alarm.' I waited for more but Helen seemed to have difficulty in continuing. Her attention was elsewhere and I wondered aloud if she was still recalling the previous night.

'Yes, I'm sorry. I'm in a bit of a daze,' she said placing her feet squarely on the rug as if to ground herself. 'I don't usually stay out so late during the week but I was having such a lovely time. I didn't want the evening to end!'

'It sounds like you had a really good evening,' I remarked, keen to know more but already wondering if she might be wanting time simply to savour the experience. Perhaps she felt that sharing it now, the very next morning, might detract from it.

'Maybe you want to just sit with your experience a while?' I suggested. She breathed a deep sigh and sat for several minutes with a smile on her lips.

'He's great fun to be with,' she said at last. 'I just love his personality and he's such a good dancer. I didn't know Bath had salsa clubs that went on so late! The time just flew by and ...' she continued to describe the evening in ever-more positive terms: the meal at a 'cheap and cheerful' café, the walk in Victoria Park, sitting outside the Abbey watching the world go by and later dancing at the underground club nearby. Though she gave little description of the man himself, it was clear that they had greatly enjoyed spending time together. I wondered if, apart from dancing together, they had become physically intimate in any way but I did not enquire. I didn't want Helen to feel any pressure to take steps that did not yet feel right for her. So I was taken aback when she said with a laugh, 'He's a very good kisser!' and I managed only a feeble, 'Oh really?' in response. She didn't go into further detail but I surmised this to have been a goodnight kiss, a romantic end to a delightful evening. Again, I allowed myself to feel some satisfaction that our work had progressed so far.

My day seemed to continue in this positive vein – perhaps, influenced by Helen's success. I often wonder how much previous sessions colour my work in the next. Or maybe it was just coincidence that my clients were in optimistic mood for the remainder of the day. John ('my life is one long tragedy') told a joke and allowed himself a fleeting smile, Christine ('I'm fat and my eating disorder doesn't help') realized it is she herself who does the eating, not her eating disorder, and Rebecca ('How can I be happy until my mother understands me?') came to the conclusion that if her mother did not understand her by now, she never would, and, after 50 years of waiting, maybe it was time to give up and just be happy.

There was one exception to this day of positive progressions. Lee was more 'wired' than ever. He'd 'met a new bird', 'been out on the town', 'boogied the night away' and ended up 'having a skin-full' with mates at a 'lock-in' at a pub down by the canal until the early hours. Having slept until the late afternoon, his day was just beginning while mine was drawing to a close. His energy was high while mine was pretty much depleted. Throughout his torrent of words, clichés and embellished anecdotes that did not hang together with any degree of authenticity, I managed only a few enquiries to ascertain whether, apart from not turning up for work, he had stayed out of trouble. If I was to believe him, he'd managed to do so. I put aside my doubt and ended the session with a smiling 'Well done' in the hope that some positive reinforcement for staying out of any violent confrontations might have some effect on his future actions. I wondered momentarily if I was becoming a behaviour therapist but Lee's non-sequiturial response of 'Whatever', accompanied by a wink, suggested that, even if I was, I was an ineffectual one.

In Helen's following session she recounted, excitedly and in some detail, her two further meetings with the man whose name I learned was Ashley. It was a joy to see her so animated and happy. It was clear she was forming an attachment to him, enjoying him when together, thinking about him between times and generally allowing him into her psyche as a mature and trustworthy male. She seemed reassured by his work credentials. For Helen, having had two fathers who'd never worked in their lives and spent even their paltry benefits on booze and the dogs, the solvency of a prospective partner was an important criterion. Ashley was Area Transport Manager for the South West region and seemed to have a deep sense of responsibility in his work having gone into quite some detail about the challenges of managing people and keeping a transport system operating smoothly. My own experience of travelling on any public transport in the South West was not one I would have described as 'smooth' but I put aside my own opinion on the matter to ask what it was that was attractive to her about this man. Clearly, my prejudice was proving harder to put aside than my opinion on South West travel. I wasn't sure that an Area Transport Manager was quite what Helen needed.

'That's a difficult question to answer,' replied Helen smiling coyly … nevertheless she continued. 'Well, this may sound shallow but there's something about the way he looks, something about his lively face and his sharp features and his wiry body. I think he's very sexy! But as well as that he's just very good company. I love listening to him. His enthusiasm comes across whether he's talking about his work or his friends or his delightful family. I don't know, he makes me feel so very alive. And I like that.'

'He sounds like a far cry from your indolent parents,' I suggested (and a far cry from my prejudicial view of anyone called a Transport

Manager, I thought to myself). 'They used you, sapped the life from you. I remember you once described your time at home as "a death sentence without the relief of execution".' Helen nodded and a tear rolled slowly down her cheek. 'I feel so lucky,' she remarked as she rose to leave. 'Lee is so very different.'

It wasn't until she'd gone that the name I'd heard her say fully registered with me. Or had she actually said 'Ashley' and I'd just caught the ending? Even if she had said 'Lee', it was an obvious abbreviation and hardly likely to be one and the same. I ran an image of my two clients through my mind. No, it was plainly ridiculous.

Yet throughout the rest of the day, I found myself making connections between them. In many ways the links were so general as to be stretching a point beyond common sense but there were some things that niggled by remaining plausible even though highly improbable. I remembered that the day Helen had told me about Ashley was the same day Lee had told me he'd 'met a new bird'. Then again, Lee was always meeting new girlfriends. The chances he had met another one on the same day that Helen met Ashley were statistically high. But I thought too of Helen's description of this man's lively face and sharp features. Could this be Lee's face – the face I describe as hollow-cheeked and angular? And how about her attraction to his enthusiasm, his amazing energy? Is this the same 'wired whippet' that so exhausts me? And could Lee in any way be the 'good kisser'? I had no idea about the latter and, perhaps fortunately, his acne prevented me pursuing any such considerations further in my imagination.

I realized this speculation was idle and ridiculous. All I had to do was check the young offender's papers. He had never referred to himself as anything but 'Lee' in the time I had known him but official reports would stick to bureaucracy and use his full name, I felt sure of it. I quickly rifled through the files in my cabinet and there it was – 'Lee Weston'. Of course, why would those 'scumbag shit-heads' (to borrow a phrase) have chosen a name like Ashley!

I was much reassured – even more so on seeing Lee again face to face in our session later that day. There was no possibility that Helen was talking of the same man. I was able to put my concerns behind me and focus fully on the spotty, hyped-up young man who sat before me. In fact, perversely (not really a word a therapist should use too flippantly), I felt a little warmer towards him as result of his failing to be Helen's man. He'd 'had a spot of bother' that day with his boss and we spent most of the session looking at ways in which he could have avoided the situation from getting so heated. At least Lee had controlled his violent temper, not lashed out, and had sensibly, if a little belatedly, walked away. We discussed how he could return to work tomorrow and reach a better understanding between him and his employer without grovelling ('I'm not kissing anyone's shitty arse' as he put it. In my mind's eye, I could see Helen shuddering and I smiled inwardly).

It was as we were discussing the ins and outs of this potential reconciliation that a disturbing thought intruded. The depot at which Lee worked was a bus depot. He cleaned the interiors when the buses returned from their rounds. I was making some vague connection with Helen's man when Lee dropped the penny for me. In his rapid-fire delivery, he said, 'Yeah, but if he gives me any lip or if he dares call me "Sunshine" or if he once, just once, puts his hand on my shoulder – like he has the right to touch me at all – I'm going straight to the top for harassment. I'll report him to the Transport Manager.'

This was too much. I'd never heard of this particular job until today and now I'd heard it from two of my clients. But what did it signify? I fell initially to the likelihood of coincidence but then the other 'coincidences' recurred and I was once again thinking of abbreviated names and energies and new girlfriends and buses and Transport Mangers – and above all, Lee's pathological tendency to confabulate.

'Do you do salsa?' I blurted out, ignorant of whether one 'does salsa' or simply 'salsas' (though not ignorant of the fact that I was, as Lee would say, 'totally out of order' in asking the question). I just couldn't stop myself. In that moment, I had become as impulsive as Lee himself.

'Salsa?' It was the first time I'd seen Lee look remotely nonplussed in response to anything I'd said. I was dreading his wanting to know why I'd asked. He'd have had every right to be suspicious and I had no idea how I'd defend my question. As it was, Lee was more impressed by my apparent clairvoyance. 'That's weird that is. Spoo-oo-ooky,' he said in a whisper, widening his eyes as if to confirm my supernatural powers. 'I go a lot. It might sound a bit poncey but it's not like on 'Strictly'… much more raunchy, if you get my drift. It's an ace way to pull – I met Helen there a few weeks ago.'

I couldn't phone Tessa. After Helen had transferred to me, she and I had agreed not to discuss her therapy, only if Helen requested it. She never had and, having already overstepped the mark with my question to Lee, I wanted to keep the boundaries as intact as I could. I phoned Christine, a trusted colleague from my supervision group, and told her the story so far.

'OK,' she said, having listen attentively and sounding reassuringly calm. 'Let me see if I've understood the situation. You suspect that two of your clients have met and started a relationship – that's difficult in itself but, not only that, you disapprove of them being together (if they are) because you feel that Lee is too young, a bit of a waster, tends towards violence and would be a disaster for Helen who has an early history with abusive men and you feel very protective of her.'

'In a nutshell,' I replied. 'I suppose I could refer him on. I was thinking of referring him on anyway …'

'Why?' put in Christine before I could continue. 'Why were you thinking of referring him on?'

'Because I felt we were getting nowhere,' I explained, feeling put on the spot. 'And I thought someone younger might be better.'

'And?' Christine persisted.

'Oh, I just feel exhausted by him,' I admitted. 'It's like working with a whippet! I know that's no reason to get rid of him but I really do feel we're getting nowhere.'

'Well, I don't think you can refer him on now,' said Christine. It was my turn to ask, 'Why?'

'Because it would be disingenuous of you,' she said flatly. 'You'd be referring him on for quite the wrong reasons – more for your comfort than his therapy. And, in any case, you're not "getting nowhere" with Lee. After all, what's he doing with a lovely woman like Helen if he's not made changes through working with you? She's no fool, is she?'

'No,' I agreed. 'She's no fool. But Lee's an accomplished con man. He's very convincing. Well, given that he's a 23-year-old ex-offender, bus cleaner without a penny to his name, he'd have to be to appear "mature", call himself "Ashley" and run the entire transport system of the South West! Not to mention his "delightful" family!'

'Hmm …' mused Christine. 'And neither has told the other they are in therapy?'

'No, not as far as I know,' I sighed. 'And I know there's no way I can get around that without manipulating the confidentiality of one of them, well, both of them really.'

'Quite so,' confirmed Christine. 'And it goes without saying that any information given by one remains solely theirs and does not get referred to with the other … I'm thinking "salsa".'

I cringed. 'I know that was a mistake.'

'It's going to be tough,' she went on, unreassuringly. 'You've got to work with each as if you knew nothing of the other. It's impossible, of course, but then didn't Freud describe ours as an impossible profession?'

'It's certainly a mad profession,' I replied. 'I feel like re-training for something totally different.'

'Oh yes?' asked Christine, sounding unconvinced. 'And what might that be?'

'Something like an Area Transport Manager?' I suggested. At least sharing the situation with Christine had somewhat reduced my anxiety.

'Yes, well,' finished Christine, 'I hope the three of you can sort out my bus timetable. It's just appalling. Keep me posted.'

I was dreading the following Wednesday but, in the event, extraordinarily, neither referred to the other. In the ensuing weeks, Helen became sharply focused on her relationship with her inadequate mother while Lee, for the first time, began to explore his early childhood experiences, especially those in which his father's brutality played a major part. This was both a relief and a puzzle to me and I confess I didn't fully engage with either of them to begin with. My resolve to hold a boundary between the current, romantic involvement of my two clients seemed emphasized by its redundancy. I found myself wondering just what might have gone on between them in the preceding weeks, curious for details, willing them to disclose some clues as to what was happening. But they were not forthcoming and as the months passed, I was mostly able to focus on the important archaic material they were dealing with. Even so, there were times when it was impossible not to see a parallel between then and now.

'She should have protected me,' asserted an angry Helen in a session in which she appeared more energized and aggressive than usual. 'She knew what was going on but she did nothing. They both betrayed the trust a child has a right to in her parents. OK, so he was not my real dad but there's still the responsibility an adult should have towards a child in his care. And she turned a blind eye to it. She was just as culpable … maybe more so as my mother.'

'You recognize your rights as a young, defenceless child,' I reflected (simultaneously applying her accusations to myself – the bystander mother, the irresponsible step-father, the irresponsible bystander me). 'A child who was powerless and frightened and needed protection.'

'I wasn't just frightened,' said Helen. 'I was terrified. Most of my young life, I was terrified. No one was there for me.'

('Like me,' I thought.)

She wept.

'He'd get angry over everything and nothing,' explained Lee. 'If I ate too quickly, he'd clobber me. If I ate too slowly, he'd clobber me. If I breathed, he'd clobber me. My dad was a time-bomb waiting to explode at the slightest excuse.'

'And you were his excuse …' I put in.

'Yeah, like I was the fucking enemy,' he shouted, his limbs agitated and twitching. 'I don't understand that. Why was I the enemy?'

'Perhaps because he envied you,' I suggested. 'Perhaps he felt threatened by you.' Again, I applied the accusations to myself. Is that why I was so intolerant of Lee? Was I envious of his youth, his energy, his years ahead of him?

'I was no threat,' he said. 'Well, not as a young kid. Not until I was big enough to hit him back.'

'Before that you were a defenceless little boy,' I remarked, encouraging him to stay with younger times. 'You needed your dad to defend you, not attack you like you were the enemy.'

'Yes,' he agreed. 'I was only a boy. I needed him on my side.'

('Like you need me,' I thought.)

He wept.

I felt I was failing them both but Christine reassured me otherwise. She pointed out that they were each addressing the formative experiences of their childhoods in a very deep and cathartic way and that they must be feeling safe enough and trusting enough to be doing this with me. She also reminded me that though they were processing the painful and distressing events they had suffered as defenceless children, both were survivors and would cope, in their own way, with whatever transpired in their relationship. I wasn't so sure about this last assertion. I feared that in some way they might simply repeat their childhood traumas, like most of us tend to do.

'Exactly so,' said Christine. 'And it's your job not to interfere or try to rescue them now – but to be there when the shit hits the fan. That's the difference. You'll be there for them – in the past, no one was.'

I knew she was right and her wise words assisted me in gaining a better perspective on my two hard-working clients. My engagement with both increased as I waited for the inevitable pay-off of their potentially transformative but ill-advised liaison.

The summer, and my usual August break, came and went. Lee's caravan holiday in Gosport, courtesy of the charity, was a catalogue of disasters from the 'crap' weather to the 'crap' food to the 'crap' people included in the ex-offenders group. Helen had decided to work through the summer as she was saving for a deposit on a flat and seemed not to mind that Ashley had had a fabulous time in

Goa (I groaned inwardly on hearing this) though she was a little concerned that someone with such sensitive skin had been to India – obviously, Lee's explanation for his lack of a tan.

I was curious about Lee's continuing invention of reality with Helen as he appeared not to be so confabulatory in our work together. Increasingly, I felt he was becoming more truthful, not just with me but with himself and I saw this as a very positive development. I guessed that the intricate web he'd woven with Helen was harder to disentangle. After all, wasn't the whole relationship based upon these fantastic threads? For him to be truthful would mean the end of the affair. I found myself feeling sorry for Lee's predicament. In many ways, he was becoming quite a presentable young man. I'd noticed his smarter clothes, his tidier hair, his clearer skin, even his calmer demeanour. He seemed more relaxed and less prone to agitating in his chair. He was not so impulsive and was managing to listen as well as to talk in a more considered way, not just blurting out a reactive torrent of words. I was beginning to like him. Furthermore, I was beginning to see how Helen could like him, maybe even be attracted to him.

But it seemed I was counting my chickens too soon. Some months later, my complacency was shattered when Helen appeared in the doorway with a black eye and a badly swollen cheek. It wasn't an immediate shattering. There was a moment of stunned horror at the sight of her face, then a tremendous crash as the edifice of my positive assumptions about Lee's development fell about me. My self-reprisals and doubts about how I had handled this situation had already taken hold by the time Helen sat in her chair. I felt sick to my stomach and sat drained and deflated like a pricked balloon.

'I was right all along,' said Helen with a fierceness I'd rarely seen in her. 'Men are just bastards – pathetic, useless, abusive, fucking bastards!'

My silence may have seemed like a therapeutic allowance of space. In fact, I simply couldn't have said a word. All I could do was keep repeating to myself – you should have known, you should have bloody known.

'Is that all men can do – lash out?' she cried. 'Is that it – no discussion, no negotiation, no understanding?'

I was feeling a little calmer and beginning to think more clearly, more about Helen than about myself and my stupidity.

'Helen, I'm really sorry about what has happened,' I said sincerely. 'This is a dreadful thing to have happened – and I can see how it reinforces all your beliefs about men. I understand that … I understand how this incident could undo all the work you've been doing to build up trust and risk getting close to men, me included. But, hopefully, if you talk about what has happened – such a devastating thing – maybe it will help you to see that this is not *all* men, this is a specific man, a man with problems. I know your past experiences have given you another perspective – and this fits so well with those – but it's still not true. Not all men are like Lee … like Ashley.' I didn't mean to say quite so much.

'Ashley? Lee?' Helen looked puzzled, and then in her more familiar, softer voice said, 'Oh, no, no, it wasn't dear Lee. No, Lee has been wonderful. He came straight round and sorted Barry out as soon as I called him. And if you think *this* looks bad,' she said pointing to her eye, 'you should see Barry.'

Barry! One of her housemates! It wasn't Lee. Thank heavens for that. I fought back a laugh – a laugh of relief and delight not just that Lee wasn't the culprit but at the thought of Barry on the receiving end of Lee's … well, formerly, I would have used the word 'violence' but, in the circumstances, 'chivalrous defence' seemed more apt. OK, so maybe his aggressive tendencies hadn't totally been eradicated but at least his motivation had vastly improved.

When I saw Lee later that day, he made no reference whatsoever to the incident and for a moment I found myself questioning again the connections I'd made. At the thought that maybe I was wrong, that there really was another Ashley or Lee, I was startled to discover that I felt disappointed. Where formally I would have been relieved (mostly for Helen) to learn they had never met, I experienced a sense of loss. Their relationship had not only become feasible, it had become a reality in my mind. They had both changed so much – Helen more assured, Lee more mature – that their individual differences, even their difference in age, had, from my changed perspective, become potential enhancements rather than obstacles. But my doubts did not trouble me for long. Lee began to speak of the woman he was seeing. She was not 'a bird'. She was not a conquest or a notch on the bedpost. She was, to Lee, a beautiful and remarkable woman who had had bad experiences of men. It was so obviously one and the same Helen he spoke of softly, tenderly, falteringly, with a respectful compassion. I felt moved by his tentative foray into an unknown world for which he struggled to find words that could describe it. He was confused. He was lost. He was overwhelmed. He was, quite simply, in love.

Epilogue

A year on and my work with them both continues. They are now having couples therapy with me – a compromise that suits the three of us. Apparently, they learned from each other very early on that they shared the same therapist but they thought it wise to hold a boundary – to make it easier for me, they said. And why should I be critical of their deception any more than my own? Sometimes, holding boundaries requires a dishonest integrity. Helen believes that our work together has helped develop not just her trust and faith in men but a belief in herself and her choices in life. Lee, or Ashley as he now prefers to be called, has come clean to Helen about his age, his job and his 'interesting' past. He says our work together has helped him grow up and experience the world as no longer peopled by 'scum-bag shit-heads' – except, perhaps, for Barry. For me, working with this disparate pair has confirmed my faith in psychotherapy so much so that I definitely won't be retraining for the job of Area Transport Manager. For one thing, the complexities of Christine's bus route would be far too challenging.

Not Playing It by the Book

I think it's true to say that out of all the clients I have worked with, those in training as psychotherapists have initially proved the most trying. Not all of them. There have been notable exceptions where the trainee's excited absorption in the theory and practice of psychotherapy has been duly matched by devotion to an intrepid exploration of themselves from the start. One might expect that this would always be the case, but others have arrived reluctantly, even resentfully, seeing their attendance merely as a course requirement rather than an opportunity for self-discovery and transformation. They see little, if anything, in need of discovering or transforming. This in itself is, of course, a self-delusional problem much in need of discovery and transformation. While I don't quite put it like that, I do suggest they go away and think about how they might want to use our time together therapeutically.

It is often these very same students who, managing to scrape together an issue or two to keep us occupied, develop a fundamentalist attitude to the theory and practice of psychotherapy. Like religious zealots, they adhere to some sort of bible – a holy book containing the commandments (though usually in excess of ten) pertaining to living the life of a perfect and blessed psychotherapist. Needless to say, in this matter of the good book I fail miserably in my practice. I neither live up to the expectations of the book nor of its keen disciples who are following it to the letter. Worse, I appear not to be a mere sinner who might be forgiven his minor transgressions but to be the devil incarnate tempting the chosen from their path. An example of this unfortunate therapeutic religiosity was a young woman aptly named Mary (with all the biblical connotations that may imply).

Making her initial enquiries on the telephone, Mary had not been at all happy when I told her I work in an integrative way drawing on various compatible approaches and schools of thought. I suppose this is akin to a Bahá'i follower talking to a Seventh Day Adventist.

'But you're on the list,' she complained flatly as if I had no right to be. 'The course has OK'd you as a suitable therapist during my training. It's a Transactional Analysis training, not an integrative training.'

'That's right,' I assured her. 'I'm on the list because I'm qualified as a clinical transactional analyst. I later trained as an integrative psychotherapist.'

'Well, I don't want any of that psychoanalytic nonsense,' she said, again without expression. I didn't inform her that transactional analysis is itself an integrative approach and owes its very existence to psychoanalytic thought. There didn't seem much point. I did, however, despite my already-forming doubts, suggest we meet for an initial interview to see if we could work together. Sometimes, perhaps unwisely, I let myself respond to challenges.

Mary didn't enjoy the 40-minute drive from Bristol to my consulting room on the other side of Bath. She didn't like my consulting room being in my house nor that it was upstairs (both 'unprofessional' in her view) nor that it had views across the valley that were 'very distracting'. She thought the sofas were too 'casual' and the wall of books too 'formal', but apart from that the room must have passed some sort of muster as she decided to end her inspection and sit down.

Mary arrived dressed funereally in grey and black. I guessed she was in her late forties and so was rather surprised when she told me she was only 30 years old. She was, as she put it, a 'housewife', married to a 'workaholic' architect who worked mostly in France; she didn't want children, lived in the prestigious Clifton area of

Bristol and grew cacti in a greenhouse her husband had designed for that purpose. Apart from this, I learned little about her current personal life nor much about her childhood history, only that she had been born in Exeter and was the single child of two academics. In answer to my enquiry as to whether she was close to her parents, she simply said 'No' and deflected from further questions about them. It was all a bit like pulling teeth and the session seemed interminable.

In answer to my question about her choice of training as a counsellor, she simply said she needed something to occupy her and chose transactional analysis because she'd read an article in a magazine in her dentist's waiting room. She'd completed a foundation year, read one and a half of Eric Berne's books on TA, found the other students rather 'immature and silly' but was looking forward to taking on a few clients in the next year and 'getting stuck in'. I don't think my involuntary shudder was noticeable but there was something definitely unsettling about this woman. Her monotone voice (to match her clothes), her dull, lifeless eyes, and her lack of emotion, apart from her constant underlying irritation, surely signified something deep and meaningful – and interesting – hidden beneath. I was intrigued by this likelihood but Mary's attitude and demeanour towards me indicated I would probably not have the opportunity to find out. I was surprised, therefore, when she said she would like to begin therapy with me as soon as possible. I'd obviously managed to get something right. Quite what, I had no idea.

'What is it that you want to achieve through being in therapy with me?' I asked, hoping to get some idea of where we might focus. I might have known it would not be so simple as I paused for her reply.

'Are you making a formal treatment contract with me?' she parried.

I should have just said yes and saved a lot of bother but I have such an antipathy to the very word 'contract' in relation to psychotherapy and the restrictions implied by such a term that I felt Mary might benefit from my pontificating. No, more honestly,

I felt argumentative and wanted to fight with her. I noticed with interest that I had such strong feelings so early on.

'There are three words there that I have some difficulty with,' I countered. 'I don't see formality as useful in the context of psychotherapy and I believe treatment belongs to a more medical model.'

'But these are in the handouts,' Mary objected. 'They're very important in contract making …'

'And that's the third word,' I interrupted.

'You can't surely have any objection to "contracts".'

'Unfortunately, I do,' I said louder and more belligerently than I'd intended. Mary looked horrified. Perhaps contract making was top on her list of commandments. She was certainly responding as if to the grossest heresy.

'It may be just a foible in me,' I continued, trying to soften both my voice and my belligerence. 'But I think contracts belong more to the legal aspects of business and commerce. I prefer to make an agreement with you about the structure of our working together – the time, the cost, the holiday arrangements – and I prefer to have areas of exploration more as intentions than contracts that might limit us.'

'It's not at all what they say on the course,' said Mary. 'I think I need a specific goal.'

'And what might that be?' I asked, realizing belatedly that I had allowed Mary to avoid my original question.

'You tell me,' said Mary. 'What should I be working towards in these sessions?'

My sigh must have been distinctly audible but, by mentally counting to ten, I controlled my breathing enough to explain to Mary that I had no agenda for what she might address in therapy, that the therapeutic space and the therapeutic relationship were here for her to use in order to reflect upon herself, her way of being in the world and those aspects of her life and personality that she may wish to explore. Of course, this was not entirely honest. Already I wanted her to have a total personality change and be someone she so apparently was not. I needed to do some serious work on myself if I was to be any use to Mary. Somehow I would have to find the 'creative indifference' that provides a safe environment for exploration, at least in the initial stages of therapy. At the moment I felt anything but neutral and I very much had an agenda.

Fortunately, I remembered enough of my TA training on contracts to attempt to retrieve the situation. Swallowing my objections, I told Mary I understood that this was all very new to her and that, while I could see how in the long run she might prefer something more specific (a 'hard' contract in the TA jargon), a 'soft' contract to fully explore what she might want to focus on was perhaps where we needed to start. The fact that I had actually used the term 'contract' seemed to satisfy Mary. In my own mind we had simply agreed to take time to explore what she might be wanting from her therapy with me. But 'contract' or 'agreement', I was pleased that the session was nearly at an end.

However, just as we were finishing, she smiled. No, that's not quite right. Her mouth smiled but the person behind it did not. 'You've forgotten to close the escape hatches,' she said coldly. To my dismay, another even more contentious, transactional analytic procedure had reared its head.

'I think we'll have to discuss that next week,' I said reaching for my diary with relief. 'It can be part of our exploration.'

'Escape Hatch Closure' is not, as one might have thought, a reference to planes or submarines where keeping escape hatches closed during a crisis would dangerously defeat their purpose. In the TA lexicon it is quite the reverse: the closure of an escape hatch means the permanent renunciation by the client of the options of killing or harming themselves or others or going crazy. My problem with all this is that I don't want to preclude these options for myself so I'm hardly likely to suggest this procedure to my clients. If I became destitute, terminally ill or decrepit I might want the choice of escape and, although I was a pacifist prior to becoming a father, I would have no qualms about clobbering anyone who was threatening the lives of my children. As for going crazy, I tend to wonder what I or my clients might be escaping by *not* going crazy. Oh dear, I thought after my session with Mary, this is going to be a rocky ride.

'So?' enquired Mary at the opening of the next session, followed by the formulaic escape hatch mantra, 'Shall I decide not to kill myself or anyone else and not to go crazy?'

'No,' I said as calmly as I could. 'But in time we can look at why you may or may not want to do any of these things.'

Behind Mary's impassive face, I could sense her rage. 'This isn't TA,' she asserted. 'I'm meant to be having TA therapy.'

This was a complaint I was to hear many times over the next few months. So much so that every now and again I would question the appropriateness of her being in therapy with me rather than a down-the-line TA therapist (of the more behavioural kind). I genuinely saw her predicament but 'Oh, no,' she would say, 'I've started now so I don't want to go over it all again with someone else.' Quite what she thought she'd gone over with me I didn't know. It certainly wasn't the details of her life. I'd learnt less of her history in three months than I'd often learnt in three sessions with most clients – at least, in terms of facts. My learning through my experience of her was another matter. I had learnt a great deal; it was mostly negative. But I had one particular question in relation to that experience: what was it that had damaged her so severely that her cold and distancing way of relating was still attempting to protect her against?

By the start of the sixth month, Mary was clearly exasperated with what she saw as my lack of respect for the TA bible. She complained bitterly that I had hardly mentioned 'ego states' and had not only done no 'script analysis' but hadn't even identified her 'drivers'. I too was exasperated, not just with her but with the Janet and John approach to psychotherapy her course seemed to be teaching. Very few of my colleagues who teach transactional analysis would recognize the rigid version that Mary was wedded to. What I was not getting across to her is that I have great respect and admiration for TA theory but that its use in a behavioural rather than relational way is not my preference. Half-way through a session of Mary's non-stop criticism of my approach, I was at the point of telling her I couldn't work with her. I felt too restricted by her need for a prescribed, classical TA approach. Surely, it was

better to finish at this point than continue any further. But I
didn't say any of this. As I thought it, as I merely let the idea pass
through my mind, I saw something in Mary's face. It was a fleeting
change – the hard, cold fixity, like an iron mask, returned within a
millisecond. But I had seen something. It reminded me of a look
that Daisy, my dog, gives as I close the garden gate behind me. The
dog realizes I'm not taking her with me. I know it's just this time.
Daisy doesn't know there'll be a next time. I know I'll be back in
ten minutes but Daisy thinks I'm leaving for ever. It's a look of
desperation and total abandonment. That's what I saw in Mary's
already-dead-again eyes.

I knew that Mary would deflect from any direct attention to what
I'd seen and what I'd surmised about her feelings. Her sensitivity
to abandonment was acute (enough to have detected some similar
miniscule change in me as I merely *thought* of ending with her),
so I put aside my stubbornness and attempted to be more what
she wanted me to be – a TA therapist. It was hard. She was hard.
Despite my use of the requisite concepts and jargon, Mary was not
to be easily pleased. Within minutes she was arguing vehemently
that my idea of ego states was not what was taught on the course.
Their model (now her model) was right. Mine was wrong. I tried
to explain that there are several models of ego states in the TA
literature and that theorists had wide-ranging and differing views
on how ego states might be conceptualized, that there were many
ways of using the basic ideas. Mary was not impressed. I suspect she
thought I was just being awkward. Sure enough, that's exactly how
I felt like being by the end of yet another heavy bout with her. I sat
speechless and morose. It was Mary who broke the silence.

'So, if my Parent ego state is, as you say, "introjected" from my
parents, what do you think they were like?' she challenged.

I rose to it.

'Like you,' I stated harshly. 'At least, like the you that you show
me here.'

'And that is ...?' she pushed further.

'That is,' I let myself be pushed, 'cold, angry and extremely
critical for a start.'

'Oh really? What else?'

Struck by the strength of my negative feelings, I stopped myself from reeling off the list of pejoratives that were forming an orderly queue in my mind. I realized I was becoming the very Parent ego state I was describing. Instead I said, 'What about those three? Do you recognize them? Would they begin to describe either of your parents?'

Mary, who had been staring at me coldly, now averted her gaze. She remained silent a while and though there was little movement in her face I could tell she was struggling with something behind that mask. I guess she found herself in a Catch 22: either she could, true to form, respond coldly, angrily and critically to my suggested description (and thus inadvertently confirm it) or simply confirm it. To my surprise and delight, she chose the latter.

'Those things describe my mother,' she averred in a soft tone I had not heard before. 'She was like that all the time with me … the little time she had for me.'

'I can hear how sad you are as you say that,' I responded, in a tone she had perhaps not heard from me before, and I watched a single tear roll down her cheek and drip onto her grey skirt.

I saw this first sign of sadness as a breakthrough but I had enough clinical experience to be prepared for the backlash in the next session. No sooner had Mary sat down than it began.

'I suppose you're pleased with yourself and your manipulation of me?' she queried, though it was more of a statement than a question. 'I suppose you think you know all the answers now?'

'I'm sorry?' I said, making sure it came out as a query rather than an apology.

'Just because you were right about my mother, doesn't mean you're right about me. You really don't know me.'

'That's true,' I agreed. 'I don't know you very well at all. I'd like to know you a great deal more than I do …'. And I was about to add 'if you'd let me' but I didn't get the chance.

'So what gives you the right to bully me in this way?' she interjected. 'You are so self-satisfied and arrogant. Or is that *your* introjected Parent ego state? Was your father as smug as you?'

As in Robert Frost's poem 'The Road Not Taken', a therapist's intervention, once made, precludes not only any another path but the knowledge of how that other path may have turned out in actuality. In supervision, I encourage practitioners to explore alternatives they might have made to the one they actually made. In doing so, they often ask, 'Would that have been better?' and I reply, 'It would have been different but whether better or worse we'll never know.' I had several options in my response to Mary and, like the therapists I supervise, I wonder what would have been the outcome of my making another choice. What if I had made an empathic response to her need to hide away behind her aggressive attack, or a mirroring response that simply reflected how I had heard her anger, or an apologetic response that confirmed her experience of me as a bully, or, conversely, a questioning response in which I sought to challenge her interpretation of events? Better? Worse? I shall never know. In the event, and purely intuitively, I chose to tell her about my father.

'Was my father smug?' I pondered aloud (aware that any smugness lay with my mother). 'No, not at all. He was a very gentle and modest man.'

Now, to a layperson, this may seem a perfectly straightforward and innocuous thing to say but to a psychotherapist it's fraught with the problems attendant on any self-disclosure by the practitioner. As I was describing my father, I was simultaneously questioning my motivation. Was I relinquishing my role as therapist to defend my father personally against Mary's attack? Was I so bored with all this battling that I wanted to shift the focus away from Mary? Was I gratifying some narcissistic need of my own – along the lines of 'my dad's better than your dad'? I thought there might be something in this last, despite the notable absence of any information about Mary's father, but it's not a familiar stance for me either personally or professionally. So why with Mary? Was it because she challenged me, the more experienced one, 'the father', who was getting it wrong and I was not only defending myself but puffing myself up in order to gain the upper hand in a struggle for power? There wasn't time for much reflection and certainly no time for answers as Mary battled on.

'Do you think I really want to know about your father?' she challenged. 'I'm not in the least bit interested.'

'I wonder why you asked?' I queried, disliking how peevish I must have sounded but determined there was something in this and unwilling to let it go. 'You asked if my father was smug. He was not.'

'I'm talking about you!' she said angrily.

'Yes, and my father,' I persisted. 'I may be smug. My father was not. Was yours?'

These two last words were apparently what we seemed to have been edging towards all this difficult time. Mary was silenced by them. She sat stock still for several minutes but I knew there was turmoil inside. Eventually she spoke.

'Is your father dead?' she asked, seemingly from left field.

I hesitated. Once more, I was aware of the issues of self-disclosure. It would be more my usual mode to explore what meaning my imagined answer may have for the client. But I hadn't been playing it by the book so far by anyone's standards, let alone Mary's. Why stop now?

'He died when I was 7 years old,' I replied, giving far more information than was ostensibly required, yet somehow I felt it relevant, I felt it to be right.

Again, there was a long silence in which I could see she was internally battling. I waited patiently, expecting she would externalize the fight. I prepared myself for the onslaught, but she chose another path. She took, for her, the road less travelled: rather than oppose me, rather than fight with me with her usual defence-by-attack, she joined me. She stepped across the void as she said 'Mine too' and let her tears erupt.

I remembered the look of desperation and abandonment she'd momentarily let slip all those weeks ago. Now, that fleeting moment (in response to my merely thinking of abandoning her) began to make some sense. She'd been abandoned by her father at a very young age. Sharing a similar loss at a similar age, I must have resonated with it, attuned to it subliminally like to the vibration of a guitar string, to account for my persistent and unfamiliar self-disclosures that had led to hers. Our similar experience had become a catalyst between us, but I was soon to learn there was one enormous difference. Mary's father had killed himself. He'd jumped in front of a train. Mary was there and she saw her father shatter. Aged 7 years old, her life had shattered too.

So much about Mary could be understood in the light of this – her funereal clothes, her premature ageing (childhood must have ended in that dreadful instant), her cold and distancing behaviour with me, her carefully chosen absent, 'workaholic' husband, her feeling at odds with everyone, experiencing them as immature and silly (they were simply enjoying living). How could she risk getting close to anyone again after such a traumatic loss? How could she risk having children, risk losing them? No wonder she craved a rulebook where everything was ordered, everything was followed safely and securely to the letter.

I guess she could have chosen insanity in response to such trauma or she could have mirrored her father's suicide. Maybe she could have killed someone – her cold, angry and extremely critical mother who blamed her for her husband's death. The escape hatches were all open and available to her throughout her life. Instead she'd chosen a grey, lifeless life (more a lonely, living death). But, after this moment of metanoia, when the two of us had really met and shared the experience of early loss (if not the awful trauma of suicide), we began the long, hard work of therapy – the revisiting the horror, the dark repetitions of feelings of despair and abandonment, the wanting to die, the hate and the desire to kill, the experience of madness, the rage and the mourning. Eventually, we could laugh together (especially when we recognized our mutually smug, internalized mothers vying for dominance) and like the brittle, harsh and spiky cacti in her greenhouse that survive the most extensive drought, we discovered there were bright buds in Mary just waiting to flower after years of dormancy.

Seven years on, well beyond the training course requirement, I said goodbye to a very different woman, a colourful, lively woman, and a very pregnant one at that. The days of the therapy bible, of the rules and regulations, were way in the distant past. She'd found herself through the rough and tumble of our relationship rather than in any theory. Nonetheless, though we never did get round to closing her 'escape hatches', I did get round to closing one of mine – at least for the duration of our work together. I contracted formally with her that I would not under any circumstances commit suicide. And this, I think, made all the difference.

In at the Deep End

Some of us find it easy to trust. Others find it nigh on impossible. While the former throw themselves into life and relationships, the latter sit on the edge and enter only warily, assuming the worst. No doubt, both have their advantages but at either extreme there may be a price to be paid. Trust is not intrinsically a good thing unless it's warranted and many could do with a bit more paranoia to assess the safety of a situation. They throw themselves in at the deep end only to find the pool has not been filled and they get injured. On the other hand, there are those who hover about at the shallow end convinced that the water is shark-infested and they never get to swim.

Pauline was not one of life's swimmers. I could tell in the first few moments of our meeting that she needed armbands, maybe a lifebelt. She was in her early forties but looked at least 10 ten years older. Her style of dress could be described as unintentional retro, several fashions having passed since its heyday in some era even long before mine. Sack-like and beige, the sole purpose of her attire was to cover and hide her body. She wore a brown headscarf knotted tightly under her chin so not a wisp of hair could be seen. Her face, however, despite a heavy mask of pale powder, could not be completely hidden and showed her to be fine-featured, even classically beautiful. But it was a scared face. Her lips slightly twitching, her eyes scrunched up as if to better scrutinize the room, she cocked her head to one side, vigilant for some ominous sound. I could palpably feel her anxiety as she cautiously sat in the chair opposite me and I felt an admiration as I imagined the courage it must have taken for someone as fearful as she to come to see me.

'Welcome,' I said with a smile, in an attempt to help her feel more at ease. 'What is it that brings you here?'

'I don't know really,' she said in almost a whisper into her lap. 'I just feel I need to talk to someone.'

'I wonder if you have some idea of what you may need to talk about?' I asked.

'I don't know really,' she repeated softly. I could see that she was beginning to tremble. She put her hands together in her lap, trying to steady them.

'That's fine,' I said gently. 'Perhaps you need some time to explore what those things might be. But I'm curious as to why now? I wonder if something has happened recently that might have brought you here?'

'Has she been to see you?' asked Pauline, as if somehow this was connected to what I'd just said.

'She being …?' I asked gently.

'My mother,' she replied sharply. 'Has my mother been to see you?'

'No, Pauline,' I assured her. 'Your mother has not been to see me as far as I know.'

'As far as you know?' said Pauline, sounding alarmed.

'I mean,' I faltered, realizing my mistake, 'I think I would, of course, know if someone had said they were your mother but I am not currently working with anyone who has made that claim.'

'She probably wouldn't!' exclaimed Pauline. 'She's far too clever for that.'

I was flabbergasted but nonetheless found myself running through all my female clients of an age to have a daughter in her early forties and who might have concealed this fact from me. Pauline's paranoia was catching. I needed to rewind a bit and get some perspective on this fragile woman's world.

'Pauline, I don't think it's likely that your mother has been to see me,' I said, sounding firm but concerned. 'But it seems really important that you help me to understand why you think she might have been here.'

Pauline hesitated, her hands working away as if wringing out a piece of cloth. She watched them for some time as if mesmerized by them. I realized she had so far made no eye contact with me at all.

'She read my diary,' Pauline explained. 'I noticed it wasn't as I left it the other day after I'd written in our appointment. I wouldn't put it past her to have come to see you first.'

'Why would she do that?' I asked.

'Because she doesn't like me doing things behind her back,' she replied. 'She wants to know everything I do. She just can't be trusted.'

I wasn't sure that anyone could be trusted in Pauline's estimation but it became quickly apparent why she might lack the necessary level of trust even for normal daily living. In the course of the next half hour, Pauline provided me with a catalogue of events in which her mother had proved less than trustworthy. She had, for example, brought Pauline up in the belief that her father had died heroically in a mountain rescue accident shortly after Pauline's birth. It was this story, embellished as it was with almost eyewitness detail by her mother, that Pauline had positively and proudly clung to throughout her lonely childhood only to discover later (from the mouth of a drunken aunt) that her father had been a nameless and casual one-night stand. Apparently, he was just one in a long line of itinerant lovers entertained by her mother. There were further less devastating but nonetheless significant tales of deceit and treachery that ranged from her mother's stealing from her purse at every opportunity and persistently opening her mail (in one instance her mother had hidden the invitation for a job interview – a job on which Pauline had set her heart) to putting a stop to Pauline's teenage dating by telling her one and only boyfriend that Pauline had a venereal disease. Pauline had had neither a job nor a relationship since. Her role was to stay at home with mother, almost like a prisoner but more of a slave.

I listened to these awful intrusions into Pauline's life with incredulity and at times I was unable to stop myself giving an audible moan of dismay. Such violations of independence and privacy smacked strongly of a narcissistic mother enviously destroying all threat of competition. Her total lack of boundaries, her ubiquitous lies and her constant, undermining criticism had left Pauline alone and lonely in a world that she could not trust. It was miraculous that she had made it to therapy, even more so that she had shared so much with me by the end of this first session. We agreed to meet the following week, but not before I made one last enquiry.

'Pauline, why haven't you left home?' I asked.

For the first time, Pauline raised her face and looked me straight in the eye as she said simply, 'She's my mother.'

I was disturbed by Pauline's visit. I felt I needed some fresh air before my next appointment and, after waiting a few minutes for her to have gone, strode briskly out along the street to the small park behind the public library. As I thought of Pauline's parting words, I remembered that hackneyed joke 'If it's not one thing it's your mother'. But I didn't laugh. Instead, I marvelled at the strength of attachment that could keep a daughter living with such a malignant presence way beyond childhood. Had Pauline taken on the parenting role? Did she feel responsible for her mother's existence in some way? Just what was it that kept her there?

As I only had a short while before my next client I could not walk for long, just once around the artificial lake, but it was long enough to consider a few hypotheses, then clear my head and enjoy the summer planting and the newly painted bandstand. I felt cheered by the fact that parks not only still exist but that they are tended and maintained so well for the public's pleasure, and without charge for admission. Surely, in this day and age when hospitals charge for parking and museums for entry, it's something of a miracle. By the time I returned to the park gates, I felt in good spirits, refreshed and ready for work. I turned for one last look at the box topiaries and, I could not be sure why, shivered involuntarily. It was more of a felt sense than anything I observed but I had the distinct impression of being watched. Somewhere in the bushes over by the path along which I had just walked, someone was watching me. I turned again out of the park gates and back to work a little less spirited. But, by the time the afternoon sessions were done, I had forgotten all about it.

Over the weeks, tentatively and cautiously, Pauline and I explored her appalling childhood (a childhood that barely warranted the name) and her malignant relationship with her mother. It reminded me of an old film with Joan Crawford (or was it Bette Davis?) as the mother but I didn't disclose this thought. I was pleased that Pauline seemed to trust me in talking about such difficult issues. Occasionally, she would allow herself to express some sadness and compassion towards herself. However, if I pushed too hard, especially if I tried to encourage an angry response to some of her mother's behaviour, Pauline's anxiety would increase. Her whole body would tremble, her voice would quaver and eventually she would withdraw into silence. It was during one of these silences in response to my heavy-handed suggestion that her mother behaved more like a despot than a parent that the doorbell rang. Pauline's trembling stopped instantly. She froze like a frightened rabbit and I, quite involuntarily, froze too.

'We'll just ignore it,' I said firmly, shaking my body out of its fixed position and relaxing my limbs.

'Do you think it's her?' asked Pauline in a whisper as the bell rang again.

The thought had already occurred to me but I reassured her, 'I doubt it. And even if it is, she has no right to intrude upon you like this.'

'She feels she has a right in everything I do,' said Pauline.

'Then she's wrong,' I asserted instantly and angrily. 'Let's carry on.'

I intended to do just that but I found I was already wondering how Pauline's mother had obtained my address. Had she been through her daughter's address book? Had she followed her here? Had she followed me back from the park all those weeks ago? It was discomforting to think of any of these possibilities. My antipathy towards this disturbed, perhaps psychotic, woman increased the more I thought of her. By equal token, my compassion for Pauline grew as she sat in silence, her already white face even paler. I reminded her that she had been describing how her mother had locked her in her room from a very early age while she entertained her male 'guests' and how sometimes she had been left for hours hungry and alone. I thought Pauline relaxed a little and that she was about to continue when the doorbell rang again. It was impossible to proceed. I envisaged that, if I did not do something, the whole session would continue to be interrupted. It had to be put a stop to now.

'Pauline, it's very unusual for me to leave the room mid-session,' I said apologetically. 'But, with your permission, I would like to go and talk with your mother and put a stop to this intrusion once and for all. It really cannot continue.' At the back of my mind, whilst aware of the doubtless ramifications of breaking the therapeutic frame, I also considered the potentially positive effect for Pauline of someone standing up to her mother. Pauline looked startled. She raised her head slightly and, unusually for her, looked straight into my eyes. I felt she was pleading but I couldn't tell whether she wanted me to act or not. I held her gaze for some moments. The doorbell rang again. Now she simply nodded and I wasted no time in rising from my chair and heading for the door. On my way down the stairs, I rehearsed what I was going to say to this thoughtless, selfish woman: something assertive, yet not abusive, strong but not aggressive. I did not want the repercussions to mean a worse time at home for Pauline. Some sort of explanation, therefore, seemed in order, some attempt to get her to understand the importance of our work. I set my face in a stern and serious expression and cleared my throat as I opened the front door.

'Parcel, sir,' said the postman, with a face as friendly as mine was hostile. 'Has to be signed for, sir, otherwise you'd have to collect it yourself. I had a feeling you was in.'

I signed the infernal machine he pushed towards me with the requisite plastic stick, unable to ascertain if my signature made any impression at all. I shoved it back at him, grudgingly took the parcel and slammed the door. Irritated (mostly with myself) I returned to the consulting room. On hearing my explanation, and further apology, Pauline's mouth seemed to turn up a little as if in a smile. I wasn't in the mood to make this observation aloud and we continued the session, in my estimation, quite unproductively.

Some weeks later, towards the end of October, I received an appointment at the local hospital for the removal of a benign skin cancer that had appeared on my nose several months before. It was a minor operation, more a nuisance than a worry for me, but it required me to take an afternoon off from my work at very short notice. It was impossible for me to offer another appointment in that particular week so it meant cancellation rather than postponement, something I regretted doing and usually managed to avoid. However, in the circumstances and knowing I would go to the bottom of the waiting list if I declined the operation, I decided little could be done but to inform my clients. I had four clients that particular afternoon, one of whom was Pauline. I was hoping to speak to her personally on the phone but after a few rings, an answer machine clicked into play. Surprisingly, it was Pauline's voice on the recorded message. She sounded different, brighter, more confident than she was face to face. If I hadn't known her, I would almost have imagined a vivacious, younger woman, a woman with an air of authority, someone very much at ease in the world. The voice invited me to leave a message after the beeps and so, without going into detail, I simply stated that I was unable to keep our next appointment and would see her at our usual time the following week.

On the appointed day, the operation went smoothly and I was able to walk back from the hospital in the late afternoon without any discomfort. I did, however, feel a little tired and occasionally stopped for a rest whenever a bench or a low wall came into view. The clocks having changed, dusk was already falling and the street lamps were flickering into their orange glow. Whether it was as a result of this hazy illumination or my tiredness, I could not tell but, on occasion, just peripherally, I caught a movement across the street a few yards behind me. Unfortunately, the lamps created shadows in the shop doorways and darkened the far side of vehicles parked along the roads so that when I turned to look at what or who was moving, my eyes took a time to adjust, and I saw only stillness. Each time I stopped, the movement seemed to stop. I tried to persuade myself it was simply a trick of the light or even something like a loose thread on the shoulder of my jacket that was causing the illusion. But a sensation similar to that which I'd felt in the park came over me. I felt I was being watched. More than that, I felt I was being followed. Involuntarily, my heart was racing, my palms were clammy, my breathing too fast: all the signs, potentially, of a panic attack. I sat for several minutes in order to regain control and managed quickly and well to subsume my nervous reactions. But I could not stop myself from turning and looking over my shoulder every few yards on the rest of my journey home despite the fact that I no longer saw any movement peripherally or otherwise.

When I turned the corner of the street, my symptoms returned. There was a figure sitting hunched against the wall in front of my house. From where I was, I couldn't tell whether it was a man or a woman but as I moved slowly nearer, making my steps as audible as possible to announce my approach, it turned its head towards me. It was Pauline.

'Michael!' she gasped as she straightened and moved towards me. 'What happened? Where have you been? Are you all right?'

I could see she'd been crying. She looked dishevelled, distraught, not at all the image I'd had when listening to her answer machine.

'Pauline?' I queried, as if I didn't know it was her. 'What are you doing here?'

'I came for my session,' she replied quietly. 'Where were you?'

'I don't understand,' I muttered, feeling confused. 'You must have been here for hours. Didn't you get my message?'

'Message?' she said, obviously ignorant of the whole situation. 'I came as usual at 3 o'clock. I've waited here since then. You left a message?'

'Yes, several days ago,' I explained. 'I told you I couldn't make our session this week. I had an appointment I couldn't avoid.' Involuntarily, I touched the side of my nose where a plaster covered the wound.

'Oh,' she sighed. It was both a sound of sympathy and of realization. 'My mother didn't tell me.'

'Your mother? She listens to your answer machine? I'm so sorry, Pauline.' I felt inept in my apology and, perhaps by way of defence, added, 'But it was your voice that gave the message. I just assumed you'd hear it.'

'It's my mother's machine,' she asserted. 'It's my mother's voice. Everything is my mother's. You should know that by now.'

Hearing the admonishment of her last remark, I was tempted to offer to see her there and then but caught myself just in time as I realized I really did not feel up to it and would only have resented the intrusion. And, after all, it wasn't my fault that she hadn't got the message. I said I was sorry she had not got it and would see her as usual the following week.

As I later thought about these events, I was perplexed as to why Pauline had waited so long for my arrival. I was baffled too as to how her mother may have known which hospital I was attending (for by now I was convinced it was she who had been following me in the dark). But the thing that struck me most forcefully was that Pauline had called me Michael, an intimacy she had not allowed herself in all this time. Furthermore, I recalled that my name was spoken softly, breathlessly, almost seductively; a possible indication that she was developing an erotic transference with me. Much as I knew the therapeutic value of this (though I do sometimes wonder at the number of unattractive, ageing therapists who seem to see erotic transferences abounding in their younger female clients, seemingly unaware of the wish fulfilment in their own transference), it was not something I had expected nor particularly welcomed, at least at this point in our work. It all seemed just too complicated. Or maybe I was more tired from the operation than I had anticipated.

Some months went by. Our sessions seemed constructive and productive. The insights she was gaining into her way of being in the world were opening up the idea that she had choices in her life. Pauline was gaining in confidence. She spoke louder, made more eye contact, and began to see herself as a woman with rights, especially in relation to her mother. Her nervous, physical agitation decreased and I noticed this was reflected in her appearance which had also become more relaxed, more contemporary. She did not cover her head with the scarf but allowed her dark, wavy hair to fall naturally down around her shoulders. She wore smart, coloured skirts and contrasting blouses that allowed the shape of her body to be revealed. She was transforming before my eyes week by week into a beautiful, younger-looking woman. She continued to address me by my first name and, when I remarked on this, told me she felt trusting enough and safe enough to let me be a real person and not just her therapist. Her trust in me and in herself was also permeating her life outside. She was no longer paddling at the shallow end of the pool but venturing further into the water. I was surprised and delighted when she told me she'd applied and been accepted for a job in a bookshop. It was not well paid but the fact that it brought her into contact with people was more important at the moment. Naturally, her mother was furious. She even took to her bed for several days in an attempt to manipulate her out of it but Pauline stood her ground and went ahead with it. There was a defiant, almost belligerent, tone in Pauline's voice as she told me this. She sounded more like a victor than a victim.

When I saw the signature at the end of the letter that arrived one morning, I felt a slight palpitation. She had even written in parentheses after her name 'Pauline's mother' as if the content of the letter might not alert me to this fact. I skim-read the vitriolic smears upon Pauline's character and shortcomings as a daughter. There was nothing that Pauline had not shared with me already of her mother's opinions of her. But her slurs upon my professionalism and my person came as quite a blow. I imagined what it must have felt like for Pauline to be on the receiving end of such damnation on a daily basis throughout her life. It was not so much the accusations of incompetence and unethical practice that got to me, as these were all quite laughable. It was more her attacks upon my person that offended me. Apart from the cruel descriptions of my physical self, my character was vilified as 'a predatory monster', 'a supercilious devil', even 'a heartless bounder' (a phrase that I thought belonged to the last century) perverting, indoctrinating, feeding on the weakness of others. I felt quite sick as I tore the letter into shreds and threw it in the bin. I had no doubt that I would not grace such a letter with a response but I was not sure whether it would be in order to talk to Pauline about it. In the end, I decided it would be an intrusion into our work. In introducing it into our session, I would be affecting the process, inserting something that, strictly speaking, was external to our therapeutic relationship. I waited to see if Pauline made mention of it which, in the event, she did not. It appeared she was quite oblivious of the letter's existence and I felt glad at my decision not to refer to it. It had affected me though. Following this letter, I noticed I checked the handwriting on any mail that appeared on my doormat. I also continued my vigilance while out in the park or walking around town, just in case I was being followed again. Sometimes, I was quite certain that I was. I started having dreams in which a dark and unidentifiable presence skulked behind the furniture in my bedroom, watching me, waiting for me.

The months passed. It was now hard for me to remember the dowdy, shy and nervous individual who had appeared in my consulting room last year. But I was taken aback when she arrived one day not only wearing a dress that I think would be described as 'off the shoulder' but one for which the term 'rainbow coloured' would be inadequate. Can there be more colours than in a rainbow?

So it seemed. She looked stunning. She looked radiant. She was laughing so much she could hardly get the words out, but then they came, 'She's dead!'.

'Your mother?' I exclaimed, asking the obvious but finding no other way to respond. 'Your mother is dead?' It was difficult for me to stop myself saying, 'I'm so pleased for you.' I just managed to bite my tongue though it was clear she was delighted.

'What a relief,' she laughed. 'I almost can't believe it. I'm free. I'm totally free!'

'Well, I think you had greatly freed yourself prior to this, but I understand what you mean,' I said, acknowledging to myself that I felt freed and very relieved too. I felt sure my disturbing dreams would cease in the light of the demise of Pauline's mother.

Between her uncontrollable laughter Pauline announced, 'I'm going away,' as if it naturally followed from her mother's death. 'I'm sorry it's such short notice but I was so excited after the funeral that I went to a travel agents and booked a month in Cape Town. Of course, I shall pay you for the month and I shall miss coming here very much but I'm so looking forward to swimming with sharks in False Bay. I go on Saturday.'

'Do you mean with dolphins?' I asked, certain this was precisely what she meant and rather attracted to the idea myself.

'No, no, with sharks!' she corrected me with another burst of laughter. 'In a cage, of course.' And following a deep chuckle, 'I mean, I'll be in the cage, not the sharks!' She was almost delirious.

'That appeals to you does it?' I enquired, trying hard to hide my incredulity and failing miserably. The session continued with Pauline excitedly telling me the thrill she anticipated of being so close to these killer creatures (noting the 'thrill' rather than 'anxiety', I decided not to make the obvious analogy with her mother) and of all the other amazing things she was so looking forward to on her South African safari.

Though Pauline's spontaneous holiday felt like an interruption to our work, it also felt right for her to go off and have some fun. After all, she deserved to be living her own life at last and I was delighted for her. Perhaps, I could even acknowledge that her

therapy so far had been a success. She'd asked what I would do in
the time vacated by her weekly session and I'd asked her what she
imagined I would do. She got it right. I would hold her in mind as
I took a walk through the park. She seemed happy with that and
I kept my word. I did think of her and hoped she was enjoying
her newfound freedom in the hot, early summer of South Africa.
Sometimes I worried about the sharks but somehow I knew she'd
be safe. She would not behave recklessly, despite her excitement. I
was sure of that. I tried to imagine the brilliant blue of the sea and
sky and the rugged landscape of the Cape baking in the heat but it
was difficult as I walked with my hands thrust deep into my coat
pockets and my collar turned up against the cold, drizzling wind
cutting across the bare park. There were no people about. At least,
none I could see. Yet oddly, that strange sensation of being watched
recurred each time I took my walk. I found myself on occasion
turning quickly as if I might catch the watcher by surprise. But
there was no one to be seen and I would hurry out of the gates
anxious to be back indoors. Yet even here, I was very much on
edge, disturbed by the sound of the mail, dreading to find a letter
from Pauline's mother though I knew well that she was dead and
buried. The phone calls didn't help. There were a few each day.
No voice, no breath, just silence. I thought to change my number
but I couldn't face the hassle. I started not to answer the phone
and let the machine field any calls. That way I could fast forward
the silences. They couldn't all be wrong numbers. I don't think
they could.

Towards the end of those four weeks, a few days prior to
Pauline's return session, I received a postcard from Cape Town. It
read: 'Michael, it's just fabulous here. Having such an adventure.
Swimming in deep, deep water. Sharks a cat's whisker away. Not
at all the heartless bounders they're made out to be. See you on
return. So much more to tell you!' I was delighted to hear that
she was having such a wonderful time but there was a tinge of
foreboding, an involuntary shudder, when I noticed the similarity
of her handwriting to that of her mother's. Would I never be rid of
that woman?

In fact, I never got to learn what more Pauline had to tell me. She did not return. A further postcard in that same handwriting some weeks later informed me she was staying in South Africa 'for the foreseeable future'. Apparently, Pauline was now one of life's swimmers both metaphorically and literally. She was happy swimming in the Indian Ocean, very happy swimming with sharks. As I walk tentatively in the local park, avoiding the path by the artificial lake, steering clear of the dark depths of the rhododendrons, I wonder about those 'heartless bounders'. It's an unusual phrase for one so relatively young.

High Spirits

I'm probably confessing to a contentious and certainly heuristic view but, early on in my practice of psychotherapy, I adopted what I believed to be a very useful 'rule of thumb' based on my experience of several clients. I discovered that when someone presented for therapy with what they called a 'spiritual' issue, it would invariably turn out to concern their sex life. Initially, I patiently followed the agenda of the 'spiritually' wounded client, sometimes for months, sometimes for years, until the topic of sex arose. Later, perhaps with the confidence of experience, but more likely with an impatient desire to cut to the chase, I would introduce the topic of sex and sexuality quite early on in our work together. Eventually, more convinced of the truth of my discovery, I would blatantly bring up the subject of sex in the initial interview. This often proved to be a profound experience for the client who, persisting in a somewhat spiritual perspective, would see my powers of accurate discernment as mystical and exclaim 'How did you know?' For me, there was no mystery involved at all. Freud had spotted this redirection of sexual energy a century ago and called it sublimation.

I don't think Luke saw it quite like that. When we met for his first session, he spent the first half telling me the story of his quest for spiritual enlightenment since a visit to India in his late teens. Now in his forties, and having undergone several immersions in ashrams, a conversion to Buddhism, a period of New Age Paganism whilst living in Glastonbury (as attested by the crystals that hung round his neck) and a recent rebirth into Christianity, he described himself as spiritually lost and incomplete.

I listened attentively until he eventually seemed to run out of steam. He looked at me expectantly, his long-fingered hands held together across his chest as if in prayer. I guess he was expecting some sort of empathic reflection of his situation, if not some hint at a direction towards a solution. So he looked rather startled when I simply enquired, 'And how's your sex life?' I noticed that he instantly laced his hands together over his crotch but voicing such an observation might have added an insult to what I could see, by his flushed face, he was experiencing as an injury. He swallowed hard before replying, 'I'm not concerned about my sex life.'

I was not convinced. Against all the best practice of honouring the client as the focus and the guide, I was so pompously wedded to my theory that I couldn't bear it to be wrong. Not that I didn't want to help the man. I'd already warmed to him, his softly spoken presentation of himself, the sadness behind those bright blue eyes, and the gangly spread of his limbs as he tried to appear relaxed in the chair. Even the crystals that mesmerizingly caught the light, casting miniature rainbows on the wall, drew me to him. But not enough for me to follow him into that ephemeral world.

I could have stayed silent. I could have returned to his spiritual life and his loss of it and his feelings about such a loss and his sense of being incomplete. I could have spent this and many subsequent sessions developing a safe, working relationship with this man. But no, like a terrier worrying a bone, I kept right on.

'Do you have one?' I asked blatantly.

'Have one ...?' he asked in return.

'A sex life,' I explained.

'Not at the moment, no, I er ...'

'Have you ever?'

He froze for a moment.

'No,' he replied as he threw himself forward and sobbed into his hands, his frail body wracked with uncontrollable shaking. There it was. It was done. The inquisitor had extracted his confession. Yet I felt no sense of victory as I watched Luke crying, only sadness that he was in such pain. And, of course, a deep desire to understand just why this attractive and healthy-looking man had lived an apparently sex-less life. But that was not to be ventured in this session. Luke shook my hand as he left, held my eyes with his, now shining bluer than before, and thanked me.

As I walked my dog by the river later that afternoon, I returned to my reflection on Luke. More accurately, I was thinking of myself in relation to Luke, especially the way I had behaved towards him earlier. Just why had I pushed him so hard to admit to his lack of sexual experience? What was it about his passion for things spiritual that had engendered such an un-empathic response from me, indeed, had brought forth my 'spiritual equals sublimated sexual' rule of thumb with a vengeance? Was it his innocence, perhaps? Did I envy such a purity of experience – so much so that I had to destroy it? Or was my aggressive reaction something that Luke was needing to elicit in me, some clue to his past experience that we might usefully work through? Whatever the attempted explanation, I was not happy with the way I had behaved.

He did not show for the next session. I wasn't that surprised given my bull-in-a-china-shop approach but I was disappointed: a sign that I wanted to work with him and was already engaged. I spent the session recalling him and his gentle fragility, pondered a hundred alternative interventions I could have made more constructively, considered a variety of reasons for his sexual abstinence and, as I would with any client who had not returned, wrote him a note saying I was sorry at his absence and hoped he would be able to attend the following week. To my relief, he left a message on my answer-phone a few days later to say he had forgotten the appointment and would be attending the next week. I vowed to myself not to make any inquisitorial exploration into his 'forgetting'. I did not want to risk his feeling assaulted again.

Luke started the next session with an apology, not for missing the last session but for 'not being quite truthful' in the first. I commented that sometimes the truth is difficult, even elusive, and that getting to his truth was what our work would be about. He seemed comforted by what I said, though maybe he was more reassured by my accepting attitude than my words.

'I have had sex,' he explained, 'but only spiritually, with God.'

'Ah,' was my feeble response as, feeling baffled, I tried to conceptualize such a thing. 'Tell me more.'

'Well, it's difficult to explain, particularly as I haven't had the experience for over a year … that's why I now feel so lost … but I used to be sexually connected to God, or perhaps it's better to say "some higher power" because I've had the experience in several religious contexts.'

'And that experience is sexual?' I checked, now intrigued by Luke's disclosure.

'Oh yes,' he said, obviously convinced that it was. I was not so sure. I was uncertain as to whether what Luke was describing fitted the description of sexual. The terrier was returning a little.

'During these experiences, do you masturbate?' I enquired as nonchalantly as I could and, when I received a negative answer, continued, 'But you do achieve orgasm?'

'Oh yes, it used to be a very orgasmic experience,' he said almost wistfully.

'So you achieve a climax and ejaculate?' I went on, already suspecting we were talking about different things.

'Oh no,' he objected. I noticed he brought his hands down and clasped them across his crotch as he had done at our first meeting.

'Did you get an erection at these times?' I ventured, already feeling that I knew the answer.

'No, no, it's not like that at all,' he replied. 'It's so difficult to explain.'

'That's fine,' I assured him. 'We can take our time exploring this. It seems very important to me that we give your concerns the careful time they need.'

'Thank you,' he said with a grateful smile.

The careful time needed was not so much in the detail as in the defining of his concerns. It was clear to me that we were unlikely to get very far while his definition of what was sexual was unclear to me and, equally, while my definition of what was spiritual was probably unclear to him. Indeed, this was a thorny area for me. My understanding of the spiritual is unclear at best, and, at worst, intolerant. There were times when I considered referring him on to someone who was more on his wavelength, someone who had some inkling of what it meant to be spiritual or to have a spiritual experience. It is something I have never had – or, at least, have not found it useful or accurate to use this term to describe. Yet, in candidly sharing this and my concerns with him, he seemed the more determined that I was the right therapist for him.

Luke's sexual/spiritual experiences were not genital. This we managed to ascertain quite easily. However, simple though it was to describe what his experiences were not, describing what they were proved more complicated. The words 'heart' and 'soul' were scattered liberally throughout our discussions, along with verbs such as 'intoxicated', 'ecstatic', 'profound', 'earth-moving', all of which may or may not be sexual depending on, in my opinion, how and where these experiences were being felt bodily. Luke assured me that they were embodied. He said he felt his heart-beat race, could feel the blood coursing through his veins, had feelings in his stomach like an adrenalin-rush of energy, became breathless, felt his mind spinning, saw stars, shook sometimes, danced at others: a description that many of my formerly drug-dependent clients have described as 'a high' which, of course, they miss and crave in much the same way as Luke seemed to miss and crave his non-medicated 'fix'. Perhaps, then, this was where we needed to focus, not so much on whether this was sexual or not, but more on his grief at the loss of such experiences.

Over the months that followed, I listened, often with sadness, always with a sense of privileged wonder, to Luke's unique story of how he had both found and lost a sense of connection with 'some benign higher power': lost too, therefore, a sense of purpose in living. With his cruelly strict, loveless and (dare I say it, in the secular sense, at least?) soul-less childhood, it became so much clearer to me why Luke, on leaving home, would venture into the realm of higher powers. The gaping hole left by his parents' lack of loving and cherishing and belonging could not, in Luke's perception, be filled by other people (he had neither the evidence nor the inkling that they were capable) but perhaps only by benign gods. Indeed, his sense of self evolved by leaps and bounds on finding for the first time a sense of being loved, being guided and guarded by something or someone in the many and several spiritual paths he took. For many years, until a year ago, he had been satisfied with his life and the path he had chosen. He had not only felt in relationship with God but in an ecstatic and complete relationship with God. He had needed no one else. Other people were inhabitants of the same world but not the object of his attention or his need. Then God had gone. Suddenly, seemingly without precipitation, God no longer existed and if there was no God, could there be any longer a Luke?

The depth and intensity of his loss was profound. It was only through the kind and generous ministrations over several months of the Glastonbury 'church' that he had stayed alive and sane enough to be advised to get some help. He had, inevitably in that weird and wonderful town, sought the services of some questionable practitioners and only came to psychotherapy following an unpleasant experience with a white witch who preferred to work naked. Luke, understandably, was having none of it. I thought better than to share my opinion on this, but I did find myself wondering whether she may have had a point. I was still a bit perplexed by the asexuality of Luke's existence.

Towards the end of our first year, through grieving and, perhaps, more importantly, through relating to another human being with whom he felt he mattered, Luke had a better sense of himself and of some semblance of meaning in a world without God. Though often finding my curiosity, and my heuristic theory, almost getting the better of me, I had not referred to sex at all since those early sessions. It was Luke who provided a suitable opportunity to introduce the subject when, once again, he was describing the feelings he used to have in his communion with God. I waited until his voice trailed off, not with tears this time, but still with a longing that touched me. I wanted him to know that such feelings, indeed perhaps even more ecstatic feelings, were still possible in more human intercourse.

'Sometimes, Luke, when you talk of these wonderful and ecstatic experiences, I'm reminded of how you might just as easily be talking about sex.'

'Yes, I remember you were confused when I first came,' said Luke. 'I suppose it was the nearest equivalent you could find.'

'In a way,' I replied, ignoring what I could have chosen to see as a gross misrepresentation (surely, it was he who had confused the sexual with the spiritual). 'I think you're right. I think what you describe as spiritual is just like a description of sex and, because you've not had a sexual experience and I've not had an experience I would describe as spiritual, we are both somewhat …'

'I have had sex,' interrupted Luke. 'Sort of …'

He paused. I was afraid he was going to say 'with God' again, which I knew would take us away from more earthly passions for the moment. But, to my relief, he went on.

'I was about 11 years old. I knew about sex, most of it from boys at school who bragged about their conquests. I somehow put the mechanics of it together over time; there were drawings in the loos that were helpfully explicit, but I remember feeling it wasn't for me. It looked and sounded all too messy and … well, I'd never been physically close to anyone, so the thought of touching so intimately just didn't … doesn't … appeal.'

'So when you say you've "sort of" had sex …'

'Yes, this is the point,' he went on. 'I tried masturbation. Again I'd heard a lot about it at school but I was shocked as my mother had always said never to touch yourself there, except to pee of course, but clearly not for anything else, least of all for pleasure. It was so confusing. I was hearing all these things at school that implied it was great but my parents told me it was wrong, very wrong …'

'How wrong?' I asked gently, intuiting that there was something more here.

Luke looked alarmed, almost terrified, but bravely continued, 'So wrong I would have to be castrated.'

'What?' I exclaimed in horror and disbelief, instantly remembering how Luke's hands had dropped protectively to his crotch on several occasions when we had talked of sex. 'Who told you something so monstrous?'

'It was my mother,' he said. 'It was the one and only time I tried to .... she caught me in the bathroom ... there was no lock ... she screamed and ran down the stairs. I jumped out of the bath and tried to pull a towel around me but she was back in seconds ... with a kitchen knife. She waved it at my genitals and told me that if I ever, ever, ever did that again, she would cut them off. And I believed her.'

Over the many years of my psychotherapy practice, I have inevitably heard some horrific stories of sexual, physical and psychological abuse yet, despite their ubiquity, they never fail to shock and sadden me. The cruelties parents inflict upon their children, in my opinion, are unforgivable. However much I may understand the generational-pathology theories that might mitigate such a view, I find I cannot and will not excuse or forgive the torture of children. My anger towards Luke's mother for what amounted in my mind to torture on all three levels rose within me like a wave from the depths of my being. It was some moments before I could speak.

'I am so sorry,' was all I could think of to say.

'Thank you. I know,' was Luke's reply.

This revelation opened a new stage in our work together. Luke's sharing of such a personal and traumatic experience brought us even closer. We were able to work through some of his long-held feelings towards his parents – his anger, sadness, despair, terror, even his never-to-be-fulfilled longing and his grief at that realization. It was not an easy journey for Luke but through his brave tenacity, he faced his past and found himself looking towards a future that held some hope. I admired him so much for the trust he put in me.

I remember writing in my notes some time towards the end of our second year of working together that my hunch concerning the sublimation of the sexual into the spiritual seemed to have been borne out by Luke's unfolding story. And, given his circumstances, who can fault such a creative solution. It was his strategy for survival and in many ways it had worked. Deprived of the vital love and affection that everyone needs, he turned to a belief in a higher power that could make up for that lack and provide a sense of belonging, of connection that had been so sorely missing. Threatened and traumatized sexually, physically and psychologically by his mother, is it any wonder that Luke forsook any hope of ordinary, human sexual contact with himself, let alone with others, and instead found what could be described as a non-genital, pseudo-sexual relationship in his spiritual relationship with God? Here, at least, was the semblance of sexuality without the threat of castration. Perhaps, one could go so far as to see his spirituality as a sexual fetish if that is how one might describe such a displacement of sexual need. Indeed, the more magical connotations of a fetish in connection with the inhabiting of inanimate objects by spirits might be seen to apply in Luke's attribution of 'having sex with God'.

As for the sudden disappearance of God, we became no clearer. Nothing out of the ordinary had occurred that we could find, no experience that would account for such a shift in perception. I had wondered if he'd dabbled in some hallucinogenic substance that had paradoxically allowed him to see 'reality'. But I trusted implicitly his denial of ever taking drugs. In the event, God's disappearance was not the only thing to happen suddenly and without warning for, in the third year of our work together, Luke returned after the long Easter break in a very agitated and excited state to tell me he had fallen madly in love, had had his first, real, genital, sexual experience and, yes, had found it profoundly, ecstatically, wonderfully, blissfully, earth-movingly beautiful. I was shocked by the speed of this (I'd assumed that we'd be working towards relationships in a slow, stage-by-stage way over several years) but I was truly delighted by the news. After listening to his excited description in which he unashamedly spared no details, I couldn't help but ask, 'So how does this compare?'

Luke looked rather impishly at me and said, 'It doesn't.'

For a moment, I felt disappointed. Then I realized, mostly from the glint of those shining blue eyes that still held mine, the ambiguity of his reply. I smiled and waited.

'There is no comparison,' he assured me. 'I have never felt such an experience in my whole life. Those feelings I had before with … well, with whatever, they just cannot be compared to what I've now experienced.'

'I'm delighted,' I said with a laugh. 'Just so delighted to see you so happy.'

'Oh yes,' he agreed. 'I do feel happy… and complete. You should have told me before!'

'And you'd have understood exactly what I meant?' I teased.

'No, you're right. It's indescribable!'

Inevitably, this was not the end of our work together. Luke's feeling so positive and complete, as in all things in life, had moments of doubt and uncertainty. I was also mindful of the speed at which Luke had 'fallen in love' and engaged with his sexuality and foresaw that we might need to work through the ensuing disappointments and setbacks that are often part of the developing process in any relationship. Indeed, I was prepared for the imminent failure of this relationship from the start as it seemed most likely that Sally, his very first girlfriend, would be one of several in Luke's delayed adolescent explorations. However, on this count I was wrong. Sally and Luke are still together and appear likely to stay that way.

I suppose in recent months Luke and I have been doing what could be described as consolidation and maintenance work in his therapy in preparation for ending at some point. We have, as yet, not fixed a date for that eventuality and our weekly sessions continue to be rich and full and apparently important to Luke. By that, I do not mean that they are not important to me, simply that their purpose is for him. The fact is I have gained a great deal from our encounters.

I'm seeing him this morning at our usual time and, for the first time, I'm feeling rather apprehensive about our meeting. I've been feeling unsettled since yesterday evening when I went for a drink with my partner and some friends out in the countryside near Bath.

It was one of those warm, sunny evenings where it feels like the day could go on for ever and night will not fall. We sat outside a pub by the river talking and laughing in this quintessentially English landscape. Much as I was enjoying myself and the company, I had a sudden urge to spend some time by myself and I announced that I was going to walk along the river for a while. I ignored the good-natured persuasions to stay and the accusations of being unsociable and assured the company I wouldn't be too long by putting in my order for another drink for the next round.

I hadn't chosen the best moment for my walk. The sun that had been just above the woods at the western end of the valley, casting long shadows along its length, was now obliterated by the one and only cloud in the sky. It seemed suddenly twilight but the heat of the long day remained and it was still pleasant to walk by the river listening to the late birds singing and seeing the occasional brown trout hanging almost stationary against the flow. The smell on the air was fresh despite the heat, a mixture of grass and moss and earthy things, clean and elemental.

I was in a very peaceful, contemplative mood and, on seeing a suitable seat-like stone, I sat down by the water's edge to watch and listen and absorb the lingering day. As I did so, the sun reappeared from behind the cloud. Though I faced downstream, the bright sunlight, catching the ripples of water, gave the impression of a sparkling movement undulating towards me. I stared for some moments hypnotized by the ripples until I felt a little giddy and glanced away upstream to relieve my eyes only to be met by the stunning sight of sunlight beaming through the trees. It split into scores of brilliant shafts that turned in the breeze like the sails of a windmill, elongated. It was so unexpectedly dramatic that I caught my breath. In that moment I could feel my heart madly racing in my chest and my blood coursing through my veins so intensely that, had I looked, I'm sure I would have seen them undulating like the river. My mind was spinning, the dizziness transformed into a rush of energy through my brain. My whole body felt flooded, intoxicated, it was shaking with some pure, energetic force. And just as suddenly it was gone and I felt totally yet blissfully spent.

As I walked back to join the others, I struggled to think how I might describe my experience. Such profound sensations are difficult to capture in words. 'Ecstatic' comes close, but it was more than that, much more than the 'high' of an ecstatic state. I think I experienced something I can only describe as erotic: as sexual, but not necessarily genitally sexual. It was sexual and simultaneously, well, the only word that came reluctantly to mind was 'spiritual'. I was so preoccupied with how to describe what had happened in words and phrases more familiar to me that I didn't notice I'd walked straight past the pub. On realizing, I quickly retraced my steps and rejoined my group of friends who continued as if I'd never left, oblivious to my disturbed state.

I didn't talk of my experience then nor even later alone with my partner. I felt it was something I needed to ponder upon more and, at least for the time being, keep to myself. Now the doorbell has rung and I hear Luke's loping footsteps down the hall.

The Audition

The female voice at the other end of the phone sounded exasperated as she repeated to me, 'Heather Hanson', and, on getting my simple 'Hello', added, 'You know, the film actress?' I didn't so I said 'Hello' again and was met by some rather heavy sighs at the other end of the line.

'You're a therapist, right?' she said, recovering eventually.

'I'm a psychotherapist,' I replied, keen to distinguish myself from a host of other therapists she may have had in mind: beauty, body, colour, aroma to name but a few.

'A shrink, right?' she continued in her clipped New York accent.

'That's right,' I replied. 'Is it psychotherapy you're looking for?'

'Could be,' she said noncommittally and then added, 'I sure do need a shrink.'

These two statements struck me as odd: the one so hesitant, the other so certain. Such a degree of ambivalence led me to think she might find it difficult to commit to psychotherapy.

'Are you good?' she asked. 'I mean, you've written books on it haven't you?'

'Well, I don't think they're necessarily connected,' I replied, already feeling uncomfortable and wondering where this woman was coming from. 'I have written books on psychotherapy. I also have varying degrees of success with my clients, sometimes none. But tell me, what is it you're looking for?'

'Oh,' she said. 'Shall I come and see you?'

Confused by this non-sequitur, puzzled by what she was wanting, uncertain as to her suitability for psychotherapy, I was overwhelmed with curiosity and I offered to meet her the following week.

Heather Hanson, a tall yet voluptuous woman in her early fifties, a cross between Greta Garbo and an elongated Dolly Parton, swept into my consulting room like a whirlwind with a mission. Before I could invite her to sit, she was over by the bookshelves lifting down various volumes, studying the spines, reading the names aloud as if to memorize them and, to my relief, returning them to their original place. A moment later she was striding across the room to the table by the window intently studying the *objets d'art* displayed upon it. She seemed particularly drawn to a group of African dancing figures and a piece of sun-bleached driftwood that natural erosion had shaped into an up-turned face. And again, having handled and almost caressed them, she returned them to their rightful positions. After a quick glance through the window, she was gliding between the furniture, her multi-coloured skirt swishing, her silk shawl billowing as she finally sank into the armchair, her clothing settling seconds behind her.

'I just like to get the feel of a place,' she explained, most probably in response to my involuntarily raised eyebrows. 'You know, pick up the vibes, get to know the space, explore the domain, familiarize myself with the environment?'

I got the idea pretty quickly. One phrase would have sufficed. I hoped this was not indicative of what was to come. I was also very much aware that her scrupulous attention had now turned to me. She slowly allowed her gaze to travel from my toes (had I brushed that mark off my shoe this morning?) to the top of my head (was that stubborn tuft of hair still sticking out at an angle?) and the rest of me in between (with a question occurring to me at each elevation as to what she might be seeing). I wondered if this was how an actor at an audition might feel under the eyes of a director but I told myself that all clients probably make this initial assessment if only in a more subconscious and inconspicuous manner. I gazed back at her as noncommittally as I could.

'Do you always wear green?' she suddenly asked.

Catching myself about to answer as if we were chatting over coffee in a hotel lounge, I said, 'I wonder what that would mean to you if I do. Might it be significant to you?'

'Significant?' she repeated as if not understanding what I was talking about. 'Oh no, not at all. No, it's just that I like to know a person, to get the feel of them, I like to see what makes them tick, you know, to get ...'

'The vibes?' I interjected, betraying, I thought, my distaste for such terms.

'Yeah, you got it!' she laughed, clapping her hands excitedly, unaware of any antipathy. 'You know, I think you and me gonna get on just fine.'

I was not so sure and was even less sure when she announced that she would love to work with me but that the therapy could only last six months. She was in the UK only until Christmas and would be filming in Hollywood in the New Year. But surely six months would be long enough, she implied, or was it implored?

I have to admit that while I put to her the likelihood that such a short time would not be productive, acknowledging that there were many psychotherapists who specialized in brief-term work and making it very clear that I was not one of them, I was nonetheless not too dissuasive of the idea. In fact, it rather excited me. Not that I knew of this woman's apparent 'celebrity' nor was I enamoured of Hollywood. Yet there was something about her by which I felt seduced. Perhaps by her grandiose display? Perhaps by her vulnerability beneath this well-practised mask? Or was it more the challenge of working with someone whose whole lifestyle might be so different from my own? Whatever the attraction, I did not make a final decision before asking what she hoped to achieve from psychotherapy.

'That's the million dollar question,' she said, taking on a grave expression. 'And I know what the answer is – I want to say goodbye to my father'.

She paused, raising one hand as if waving goodbye, the other moving to dab her eyes, seemingly moved by what she had said.

'He's dead, you know, he's been dead and gone a long time. But he's here,' she moaned, striking her chest dramatically. 'The bastard is still here inside of me and I want him out.'

Despite Heather's melodramatic performance, I thought I detected a grain of authenticity, a small window through the façade of years of acting and playing roles on and off stage that gave me a glimmer of the inner suffering of a real person. I suspected some early trauma and was not surprised when she revealed that her father, himself an actor, had sexually and psychologically abused her from a very early age. I knew that six months was not going to be enough time to work through these dreadful experiences and I told her so.

'But we can give it a shot, can't we?' she appealed. 'I mean, we can make a start and see how it goes. I need to do this now. How about it?'

'Why do you need to do this now?' I asked, thinking to persuade her to wait until she could devote more time to herself, but she was having none of it.

'It has to be now,' she said firmly. 'My future depends on it, my career depends on it. It's getting in the way of my acting and I'm damn well not going to let him do that to me, not on your life!'

She sounded determined and I took that as a sign that there may be some mileage even in short-term work. Against all my other better judgements, indeed, against my usual preference for long-term work, I agreed to see her twice a week for the next six months. I think I was tempted by the challenge of finding the essence of a real person beneath such a dramatic and formidable adaptation.

And a challenge it was. There were times I regretted my decision. Besides the tedium of her tautological phrases, I felt we were chipping away at concrete with a very blunt instrument. Not that the experiences she had had at the hands of her father were not available to her, and not that the details she seemed to remember were not horrific. It was simply that, over the four months we had already been working together, she told these stories with such dramatic vocal projection and such practised enunciation that it was hard for me to feel impacted by them at all. It was as if I was part of an audience – sitting in the back row of the upper circle of a theatre at that. Her emotional expression, complete with wild gesticulations, deep guttural sounds and even profusely watery eyes, stayed distant on the imaginary stage on which she performed and failed to move me in any way.

Despite the difficulty on my side, Heather seemed to be fully impacted by me and particularly by my words. She would often begin a session by recapping on what I had said previously, often word for word, as if it had meant something profound for her. This gave me hope that something was getting through and that maybe some change was occurring internally if not yet externally.

Just before a session one day in November, as I sat pondering on our work, mindful of the little time we had left, I realized that Heather was likely to continue performing and that I was likely to remain simply her audience for the remainder of our work together. Once this fact had fully registered, I decided that this was exactly where we needed to stay but that we must utilize it differently. The performance on stage needed complementing with another character. On an impulse, I quickly moved an armchair and placed it adjacent to the one in which she normally sat, not too close but close enough that two people might easily hold a conversation on stage. On entering the room in her usual grand manner, Heather noticed the rearrangement instantly.

'That's not right,' she remarked, already attempting to move the chair back to its usual place. 'I might need a hand here …'

'No, Heather, leave it there a moment, please,' I requested in a way that even devout non-directive therapists sometimes do. 'I have a suggestion to put to you.'

'Oh really?' she replied, raising her eyebrows in what I thought was interest but which turned out to be uncertainty. 'Is it kosher? I mean, is it the sort of thing a shrink normally does? Is it usual to make suggestions? Would another shrink be doing this with me?'

I was struck by her concern about the legitimacy of my intervention rather than showing any curiosity as to what I was going to suggest. I was about to remark on this when she seemed to realize herself that her attention to protocol might be unwarranted or, at least, premature.

'Well, whatever!' She exclaimed, interrupting me. 'I guess you wouldn't suggest anything without therapeutic potential. So what's the idea?'

I chose to move to my suggestion rather than explore her earlier response. I was keen to avoid a diversion at this time.

'I'd like to suggest that you talk to your father.'

'To my father?' Heather exclaimed almost recoiling in melodramatic horror. 'I'm not sure I could do that. I doubt I could bring myself to talk to him, that bastard …'

'Tell him that,' I interjected. 'Tell him how difficult it is to talk to him. Imagine he's sitting there in that chair.'

Heather turned and looked into the empty chair. She stared in silence for some time and, for a moment, I thought she was going to bottle out of the idea. But then, with a sudden burst of energy, she leant forward in her chair, gripped the arms as if to gain support from them and screamed, 'You bastard! You sick, perverted, low-life bastard! You mother-fucker! No, you daughter-fucker! How dare you do that to me! How could you treat your own daughter like that?'

She railed and ranted and screamed and yelled and hit the arms of the chair for a full 10 minutes. She looked like one possessed. Her hair fell over her eyes, her tears soaked her silken dress, her eyes bulged, her nose bubbled with snot and beads of sweat trickled from her brow. She was not acting. I don't think she was even aware of my presence. It was only after her body had collapsed into the chair that I ventured to speak.

'You clearly loved him so much,' was all I said. It was enough.

'I really loved you, daddy,' she whispered quietly to the chair before falling back into the cushions and letting her body convulse with sobbing, her head thrown back, her up-turned face streaming with snot and tears and sweat. She looked a wreck and probably knew it but she did not try to hide herself at all.

We sat in silence for a while. When, eventually, she looked my way, I smiled and she returned a genuine smile for the very first time – with me, at least, but perhaps for the first time with anyone in her adult life. We had made an authentic connection both to the past and with each other in the present.

'Thank you,' she said softly as she walked to the door at the end of the session. I noticed she didn't even stop to wipe her face or re-arrange her clothes. I suspect she didn't care.

In the final few weeks, Heather seemed to me to be a different person. I don't mean that all her defensive and dramatic presentations disappeared – she was still Heather Hanson, the actress – but there was something softer, more approachable about her which, on occasion, enabled us to meet as two people without pretence. She talked of her father's abuse and cruelty with a genuine expression of emotion and I was able to empathize both with that little girl who had been so badly treated and with the woman who sat before me now, a woman who had survived at the cost of being herself. And yet, what a clever way she had found of turning an adaptation to advantage. What better way than to follow a career in which her ability to pretend was rewarded with fame and fortune? I knew there was still much work for her to do but I felt she had begun to say goodbye to her father and I hoped she could move on more authentically, at least in her off-stage life.

In our final session, Heather and I spent some time in summarizing the work we had done together and in sharing our mutual appreciation of each other's participation in this endeavour. I was surprised however that in the last half of the session, rather than stay within this more interpersonal dialogue, she asked several hypothetical questions that seemed to have great importance to her. What would I have done if she hadn't turned up for a session? What if she'd threatened to walk out? How would I have responded if she'd asked me to hold her? Would I have talked to her on the telephone if she'd phoned between sessions? And so on. I pointed out that she had done none of these things and wondered if she was checking one final time that her trust in me was well founded, that if I answered her questions 'correctly' and consistent with her actual experience of me, she could confirm the boundaries I had held and carry them away with her. She said she wasn't quite sure but expected I was right. We said our goodbyes and wished each other well for the future. She thanked me yet again as she moved to the door.

'You've helped me enormously ... more than you may have realized,' she said and, on that tantalizing note, was gone.

I imagine that clients often consider themselves forgotten by their therapist once their therapy has ended, but they would be wrong. I don't think I am alone in finding myself reminded of a past client by some particular situation, a certain phrase or mannerism or even just thinking about them in the course of a day and wondering how they are and where they are in their lives now, however many years on. I thought of Heather each time I used the empty chair with another client. I was also reminded of her when I heard a female New York accent or caught sight of a silk shawl billowing behind a woman in town. However, it's not often that I hear mention of my clients by name but this was the case when, some 18 months later, I was dining out with a friend. In the course of our varied conversation, he mentioned a film he'd seen recently called *The Silent Past* in which Heather Hanson starred. He highly recommended that I should see it as, in his opinion, it dealt with psychotherapy in a way no Hollywood film had previously managed to achieve – with what he described as 'eerily realistic authenticity'. Apparently, it had been nominated for several Oscars, as had Heather in the leading role. Of course, I made no mention of my knowledge of Heather nor did I want to give away our professional relationship by asking too much about her performance in the film but my curiosity was aroused. So much so that later that evening I am to be found seated in my local cinema watching the opening credits of *The Silent Past* – yes, starring Heather Hanson – with a sense of excited anticipation.

She looks stunningly beautiful as the vivacious, middle-aged wife of a powerful business tycoon who, away from the public gaze, treats her like dirt and subjects her to all manner of psychological, physical and sexual abuse. The tension between their public and private lives is powerfully held throughout the opening scenes and I find myself forgetting this is Heather Hanson in a role, so totally absorbed am I in the plot. Even when, almost an hour into the film, she visits a psychotherapist for the first time, it's several seconds before I realize I've become distracted and unsettled. The camera, in close-up, pans slowly across the books in a shelf-lined wall and, as the titles come into focus, I realize their familiarity and the reason for my discomfort. These are my books. At least, many of these books are the same as mine.

But my familiarity with the books is only the beginning. My unease increases as further similarities appear. The camera sweeps slowly from left to right across the room, taking in a group of African dancing figures, then a piece of driftwood that looks like an upturned face, now the other furnishings and materials. It is my room. These are my possessions. With such attention to detail, it's hard for me to believe this is just a film set. I feel most peculiar, almost faint, as I sit and watch my personal environment displayed for all the world to see. I am in a state of shock by the time the camera reaches an armchair in which the back of a figure can be seen. He is wearing green. A tuft of hair sticks out at an angle from his otherwise well-groomed head. It can only be me. That is my outline. Sitting watching in stunned amazement, I involuntarily raise my hand to brush down my stubborn tuft of hair just as the figure on screen performs the same action. The camera momentarily moves in behind the man, his silhouette filling the screen. Now it zooms in over his right shoulder to Heather sitting opposite, tears running copiously down her cheeks, looking distraught and beautiful in her billowing silks. There is heartfelt anguish in her eyes. Straight to camera, but as if to him, as if to me, she says the words I am already dreading, 'I want to say goodbye to my father'.

Whether *The Silent Past* was a good film or not, I am unable to judge. It certainly had the 'eerily realistic authenticity' my friend had claimed. But watching the enactment of our sessions on screen was too disturbing and upsetting for me to appreciate the film's artistic merit. Heather, I know (how could she not be?), was brilliant. She played the part of a therapy client with great conviction, letting herself be held in the therapist's/camera's gaze as she gave voice to her silent past, revealing little by little, as if from a safe distance at first, the story of her abuse. Eventually, she talked to the empty chair with the same depth of emotion, passion and pathos that she had expressed in my room. Even her sweat and snot and tears looked real. The traumas of her childhood had the audience audibly aghast and I could feel they were rooting for her as the film progressed. They even applauded each time she asserted her strengthening confidence and by the time of her eventual liberation from her tyrannical husband, many were on their feet.

As I walked home that evening, I felt a combination of admiration, anger and amusement. I re-ran the six months of our acquaintance over and over again. So much slotted into place: Heather's initial phone call, her so definite need of a shrink alongside her hesitance about her need of psychotherapy, her attention to the details of my books, my clothes, my room, her keenness for the protocol of therapy, the memorizing of my words. I felt admiration for her striking performance both on and off screen. Almost simultaneously I felt anger at her dissemblance. It was obvious to me now that our very first session had been merely an audition. I felt amused by the fact that I got the part and that I unwittingly played it for the rest of our work while Heather undertook her improvised rehearsal.

My colleagues in my supervision group were even more amused when I told them what had transpired. Teasingly, they suggested I put in a claim for royalty payments or at least some compensation for the infringement of copyright. Along with jokes about casting couches, they made ribald remarks implying I'd slept with Heather to get the part. In my defence against their attempted humiliation, I pointed out that in previous discussions of my work with Heather, no one in the group, any more than I, had suspected her duplicity. Having said this, the tone of the group became more serious and I explored in some detail the work I had done with her. Despite the overwhelming evidence that I had been used simply to gain insider knowledge for her film, I still had a nagging doubt that this was totally the case. I couldn't accept that those moments of seemingly true and deep emotion, even more the moments of what I experienced as real meeting, could have been entirely sham. Or had I simply been doing this job too long?

I heard the film received many Oscars and that Heather was awarded hers for Best Actress but it was many years later before I learnt any more of Heather Hanson the person. In her 60th year she wrote an autobiography entitled, as her now famous and somewhat cult film, *The Silent Past*. She sent me a copy in which she'd inscribed the words, 'more than you may have realized ...' by which, at first, I felt quite touched but then confused. I found myself wondering if this was a joke and, if not, how she could refer to me in this way given that she had so shamelessly exploited me. I turned over the book and looked at the photograph on the cover. I saw in her eyes, as I had all that time ago, a vulnerability beneath the showy smile, an authenticity that could not be hidden. I read the book.

And now it does all slot into place. In the early chapters, the ones I was most interested in, she writes extensively of her childhood. It is the same terrible childhood she brought to therapy. It is the same dreadful childhood presented by her character in the film. In her reflections, she recognizes and acknowledges that brave young girl who fled from the cruelty of her father into a fantasy world, a world in which she could be whoever she wanted to be – but never her self – a world made up of stages and film sets, of amazing characters and even more amazing adventures.

When the book reaches her adult years, she writes mostly of her parts in plays and films and of those actors with whom she starred. Most of the names meant nothing to me but there was the occasional celebrity I had seen on screen. In general, I was able to get a better sense of just how hard she had worked and to admire her courage and tenacity throughout her early chequered career. I was also struck by the number of times she had acted with her father: a collaboration that was clearly fraught with difficulties for her. Though she confesses to seeing herself as a star from an early age, she also candidly admits to never feeling she had genuinely given a performance that might warrant such a claim, not until *The Silent Past*. And, of course, this was of more interest to me.

What she had failed to mention to me, and what I think few people knew apart from the director and producers, was that the film was partly based upon her life and was written by her. Only in this autobiography does she go public about the film's authorship. At the time, she wanted her personal origins to remain the fantasy her followers seemed to want – the carefree, happy father and daughter who shared a love of acting. Her film was a way of confronting this deceit but six months prior to filming, she wanted to pull out. She just couldn't go through with it. She couldn't act the part of herself. She couldn't face the spectre of her father. She asked the director to find another actor to take her place but, astutely, he persuaded her that only she could do it. It was he who suggested she see a shrink across the pond. It was she who rewrote the film to include her experience in therapy and to use it as a vehicle for her unfolding story.

At one point, touchingly, she writes, 'I cannot thank enough the kind Englishman who helped me give voice to the past and bid it goodbye.' But she has.

Dream On

(First published in *Tales of Psychotherapy*, Jane Ryan (ed.), Karnac, 2007)

Cheryl's problem? Aged 38 and single. My diagnosis? A delightful romantic. Her belief? One day my prince will come. My prognosis? He won't. Her hope? That therapy will help find him. My therapeutic objective? Get real.

It wasn't that Cheryl was short of suitors. They'd practically been queuing up at her door since she was a teenager. This tall, lithe, dark-haired, sultrily beautiful woman could have had her pick from hundreds of adoring men. Her physical beauty was equally matched by a warm and attractive personality. She was witty, intelligent, thoughtful, fun-loving, considerate, responsible, well-read, socially and occupationally successful and, despite all this, remained modest. She was well liked by all who came into contact with her, including me. And yet, she was one of my most challenging clients. Her belief that somewhere in the world was Mr Right – no, that's not quite it, more her belief that somewhere was the *one and only* Mr Right for her in all the world – was as intractable a conviction as I have ever met.

A formidable businesswoman, an articulate host, a sensible and trustworthy friend and yet, in her relationships with men, Cheryl was totally unrealistic. Brought up on fairy tales, the Disney versions at that, her romantic dream of the man she would meet and marry was, as I so often told her, as likely as learning to fly.

Inevitably no man she met came remotely near to her ideal. How could he? This was a fantasy man. He didn't exist.

'No, he wasn't right,' she would say in her naturally sensual voice. 'I know you think I'm stupid, but I could tell from the moment I met him that he didn't fit the bill. I just knew it.'

'I don't think you're stupid,' I would reply. 'Far from it. It would make more sense if you were. But you have just described, as so often you do, a handsome, intelligent, articulate, considerate, caring, eligible man whom you dismissed within the first few seconds of meeting.'

'That's when I'll know,' she would insist.

The fairy tales were, of course, an expression of a much deeper longing. They provided a loom around which she could weave her desperate fantasy: a fantasy that contained all her yearning for her lost father. He had died of cancer when Cheryl was four – an age rife with oedipal wishes to usurp mother's place and marry father. Winning the oedipal battle can be disastrous, but losing it before it can be lost with dignity can be even more profound, as I believe it was for Cheryl. She had few actual memories of him but naturally had formed an idealized picture of what he was like. Certainly, he was attractive, as evidenced by the photographs she showed me. 'Tall, dark and handsome' would describe the father as equally well as the daughter. But as to his being the all-powerful, all-loving, all-giving prince of her fantasy, I could only try to disillusion her by making him real, by making him human, with human frailties.

Rationally, she could accept this but it did nothing to shift the idealized fantasy she clung to on a more emotional and primitive level. I realized this shift may only come about if tackled within the transference and I attempted to explore this with her one day when she asked me if I liked classical music.

'I know your father liked classical music,' I replied, avoiding the surface level of the question. 'I wonder if there's a wish on your part for me to be like him?'

Cheryl smiled. She hesitated before saying anything, as if she was choosing her words carefully.

'I know what you're implying,' she said, still smiling. 'You think I may see you as my father. But I have to be honest …'

'Yes, do,' I encouraged.

'It's just that you're not handsome and you're too old.' She was not smiling now.

The first judgment I had to accept. Handsome was not a word I would use to describe myself. I had long ago agreed with my partner and friends whose description of me as 'interesting looking' seemed more accurate. I had few illusions on that score. I was, however, about to challenge her second judgement when it occurred to me that she was right on that score too. I was chronologically old enough to be her father and certainly not too old! But her actual father had not grown old at all. He had remained the age he was when he died. He would always be the thirty-something father of the photographs.

'Your father remains young in time for ever,' I observed. 'You are about his age now. But you will age while he will not.'

'That's right,' she said, now smiling again. 'I'd better hurry up.'

'To find your father?' I asked.

'No, to find a man as good as my father.'

'That's a tall order,' I said rather sombrely.

'But it will happen,' she replied with her usual optimism.

And so we continued. My challenge to disillusion her, to help her 'get real' and engage with a man who was not based in fantasy was becoming more urgent as time went on. We had already worked together for two years. I had my own rather negative fantasy of Cheryl growing old without a partner. Perhaps, she was more influenced by her mother's chosen path of a long widowhood than her espoused desire to have a man in her life.

Then she had a dream. This was significant in itself as Cheryl rarely remembered her dreams and never in such detail. Usually they were impressionistic shades of shapes and colours, wordless but full of feeling and longing. This was quite different in its narrative structure and its clarity – at least its dream-world clarity of story, if not of meaning.

'I'm out in the countryside walking with two people, a man and a woman, along the banks of a river,' she told me. 'I'm carrying a picnic basket full of food and wine. When we come upon a field of

red poppies, we sit to have our picnic. We're laughing and joking
and having lots of fun but I'm aware of being watched. I think
I hear someone in the long grass, and I jump up. As I do so, I knock
over the picnic basket which spills its contents on the ground. I
look in the long grass and find a large green snake looking at me.
I realize this is what has been looking at me all along. It turns and
disappears into the grass. As I repack the basket, I notice there's a
letter addressed to me on top. I start to open the letter – but I wake
up before I can read what is says.'

'How did you feel on waking?' I asked, noticing there was a
marked absence of feelings in her reporting of the dream.

'I guess, I felt disappointed,' she replied. 'I would have liked to
know what the letter said. It's a bit tantalizing, like the dream was
leading to this point and then didn't come up with the goods.'

'That sounds familiar,' I suggested.

'Well, yes, I suppose so,' she concurred. 'It feels similar to how I
feel about the men I meet. I'm hopeful, then disappointed.'

'Tell me what you make of the dream itself,' I encouraged her.
'What do you think it's saying to you?'

'I'm not sure,' she said, reclining further back in her chair to
ponder on this. 'Apart from the ending, I enjoyed the dream. I
think I felt happy in it. I think it was saying something positive.'

'So how are you understanding it?' I probed. 'For example, who
are the two people? What do they represent for you?'

'In reality, I don't know them. They're not people I recognize,'
Cheryl explained. 'I know we've talked about my masculine and
feminine aspects. I suppose they might represent those. I felt very
in tune with them, enjoying them. I felt very safe. Do you think it's
something to do with feeling balanced?'

'That's possible,' I agreed. 'But what also occurs to me when you
say you felt safe is the safety a child might feel with her two parents.'

Cheryl instantly looked tearful.

'Oh yes,' she cried, a tear trickling down her cheek. 'That
feels right. Yes, it was a lovely feeling. It felt like this is how it
should be.'

I waited for her to cry some more. This interpretation seemed
to have moved her deeply and I did not want to interrupt her. In

a while, she sat up again and wiped her eyes with a tissue, clearly signalling she was ready to go on.

'We're in the countryside walking along a river bank,' she recounted. 'It's very beautiful.'

'What about the river? Do you notice anything significant?' I asked.

Cheryl closed her eyes, the better to recapture it. 'It's flowing away from us, It's quite fast and there are bends where we can't see where it's going until we turn a corner. It's deep in places while in others I can see the bottom. I guess it's life really. I think it's my life stretching out ahead of me. And, of course, I don't know what's coming until I'm there, until I'm round the bend!'

I laughed with her at her Freudian slip. We could have taken it as a serious suggestion, perhaps explored the 'madness' of her Prince Charming quest, but it felt more like a moment of intimacy between us as we shared the humour, rather like she did with the two others in the safety of her dream.

'So it may be that your dream sees you walking through life with your parents and you feel that this is how it should be,' I summarized so far. 'And the picnic basket?'

'Oh, that's full of goodies!' Cheryl exclaimed, apparently delighted by the thought.

'Goodies?' I repeated.

'Yes, it's full of good things!' she continued in her excited fashion. 'It must be saying that life is good. At this point on the journey through life, everything is good and as it should be. And then we see this beautiful field of poppies, bright red, masses of them and that's where we stop.'

She hesitated as she seemed to realize what she had just said. I wondered aloud if she had meant that's where the 'we' stops, that the family is ending there. She nodded in assent.

'But no,' she revoked emphatically, quickly contradicting her nod. 'It doesn't stop there. We have the picnic. We laugh and we joke and we have a wonderful time.'

'Surrounded by a field of poppies,' I reminded her.

'Yes, those beautiful poppies,' she sighed. 'Those blood red, danger red, death red poppies.'

'And …?' I urged her on.

'And, despite the fun, I have this feeling of being watched,' she said softly. 'There is something lurking, something waiting in the long grass.'

She paused for just a moment and then with certainty stated, 'The snake is death.'

I let the words hang in the room between us. I felt this was so important for Cheryl. It seemed to me that, after all this time, the dream was bringing her to the reality of her father's death and, maybe for the first time, to feel the full impact of that loss. Perhaps, after this, she could really grieve and move on into the reality of living with human partners rather than an idealized ghost. But then she seemed to doubt her interpretation.

'"The snake in the grass!"' she laughed. 'But it wasn't threatening. There was nothing devious about it. It was just looking and it did me no harm.'

'That's true,' I confirmed. 'It did you no harm.'

'Don't you shrinks think that snakes are sexual symbols, phalluses?' she suddenly asked.

'Cheryl, these are your symbols,' I replied. 'There are many possibilities. What makes most sense for you?'

'I think that's what it is,' she said, but seemed to be convincing herself rather than sounding convinced. 'It's sex. It's something to do with a relationship.'

'Maybe it is,' I said. Having assured her of her ownership of the dream and its symbolism, I did not want to impose my own conviction of her first interpretation – though, I must admit, I hoped she'd return to it and was relieved when she did.

'I guess I just don't want to see it,' she said. 'I think I'm wanting to hold on to the positive feelings I had about the dream.'

'Those came later,' I reminded her. 'Your initial feeling was disappointment. Maybe you are trying to avoid the disappointment of your dream – a dream that seems to be merely emphasizing the reality of your loss. We're both avoiding the upsetting of the picnic basket even before you see the snake.'

'Yes, you're right,' she said, now looking sad again. 'It was upset. Everything spilled out. All the goodies were spoilt!'

She wept profusely. I suspected the profundity of the dream had hit the reality of her childhood and its impact was devastating. I could do no more than sit with her as she sobbed. We were nearing the end of the session and, though I was curious about the unopened letter of her dream's pre-waking moment, I considered it more important for her to stay with her grief.

After she'd gone, I went over the dream again in my mind. It contained all the elements of her young life, the pleasure, the hope, the future, the security she had had and still craved – and the dashing of that hope, the frightening destruction of the family through the impending death of her father. It seemed to me that Cheryl's unconscious mind had considered the timing right to let her feel the despair of her loss and be done with fairy tales. Like the ancient tribes who would have seen the snake, and its shedding of skin, as a symbol of rebirth, I privately held the view that this would be a major transformation for her.

I was prepared for Cheryl to enter a period of mourning, even of depression following our session on the dream so I was surprised when she returned for our next meeting looking cheerful, indeed, looking radiant. There was something about her that sparkled. Her already beautiful presence had now an extra intensity and passion. I sat and waited as neutrally as possible but I was immensely keen to learn of this sudden – too sudden? – transformation of energy. I was also concerned. After all, it is not uncommon for people to avoid painful feelings by 'fleeing into health'.

'It's happened!' she announced even before she had sat down, almost beside herself with excitement. 'I can hardly believe it but I've met the love of my life!'

My heart sank. This news confirmed my worst fear that Cheryl might again avoid her grief by hiding in her childhood fantasies. Now, it seemed she was deluding herself further in the belief that her prince had really come. I wondered how to approach this. It's hard to have the task of disillusioning someone who thinks they have just fulfilled the quest of a lifetime. I hoped something might present itself in the session that would enable me to gently instil some reality. For now, I was curious about what had happened and I knew I was about to be told.

'It's all so amazing really,' she laughed, the words just tumbling out. 'I nearly didn't go and if I hadn't, well, I'd never have met him. But I did and we met and, gosh, he's so right. Oh, and by the way, the snake must have been sexuality. He's very sexy!'

At least she had remembered the dream. There was some hope in that but I was none the wiser about what she was telling me. Her euphoria had totally obliterated her usual eloquence. She may have seen my puzzlement as she took a few deep breaths and calmed herself.

'My friend John had invited me to go out for a meal with some friends of his,' she explained in a more moderated tone. 'In the event, John was ill. I was going to cancel but John insisted I would like this couple, Simon and Catherine, and persuaded me to go ahead anyway. So I did and they were lovely. I felt really at home with them, as if I'd known them all my life. We went to the Café Rouge on River Street and had a wonderful meal and we talked and laughed and joked. It was such a lovely time.'

Her delight in her story could have been infectious but it was not delight that I felt as I sat and listened. I had a strange sensation which I find hard to describe. Anxiety? Fear? I'm not sure. I was already surmising that she'd fallen for the man of the couple she dined with – and all the complications that might entail, not least, the oedipal triangle she might be re-creating. But it was more than this. There was something in this story – so far positive and innocent-sounding – something that left me feeling uncomfortable. I noticed the hairs on my arms were rising. But I couldn't understand my strange reaction. I could only observe it as Cheryl continued.

'Well, we got to the end of the meal and I'd fumbled about in my bag to find my purse. But, sweetly, Simon insisted they would treat me. I needed the loo, so while they were waiting for the waiter to come, I got up – quite forgetting my open bag was still on my knee. God, I felt so embarrassed! The contents spilled all over the floor, just everywhere. I really shouldn't carry so much junk around with me. Anyway …'

But I did not hear what followed. The hairs on my arms were standing almost erect from my skin. The falling bag had fully alerted me to the cause of my previous subconscious disturbance. I re-ran Cheryl's story through my mind: a meal with a couple she didn't know, River Street, Café Rouge, the fun and laughter, feeling at home. She was telling me the dream all over again.

'Are you alright?' she was asking me, sitting forward in her chair with a look of concern.

'Cheryl,' I faltered, struggling to bring myself into the room. 'I'm so sorry. I was distracted by several thoughts in response to your story. I wonder ... well, I ...'

'You mean the dream,' she interrupted.

'Yes, your dream,' I said, rather surprised at the matter-of-fact way she referred to it. 'Have you, I mean, do you see ...?'

She interrupted me again as if to save me from my hesitancy, 'Yes, it's the dream come true. You seem surprised.'

'Well, it is rather uncanny ... the couple, the river, the poppies,' was all I could think to reply.

'Shall I finish the story?' she asked in a somewhat teasing manner. She was clearly as unfazed by it all as I was disconcerted. She went on anyway. 'I knelt down to gather together the contents of my bag – which, of course, is the picnic basket. But no, I didn't feel that everything was spoiled. It was just an accident. No big deal. In fact, I was laughing as I packed the bag again. Then someone was helping me, someone who'd been sitting at the table behind me all evening. I looked up at this green-suited man, into his green eyes – yes, the snake, the beautiful snake – and I knew. I knew in an instant, as I've so often predicted, that this was the man I would live with.'

'You discussed this possibility together?' I asked, probably sounding as tetchily disbelieving as I felt.

'No,' she replied calmly. 'We didn't talk at all.'

I was tempted to say, 'I suppose you just walked hand in hand off into the sunset!' but I stopped myself from losing my professionalism in such a swipe. I had, however, lost control of my feelings. Why was I so irritated? Why did I want to destroy the very thing my client had come to therapy for in the first place? Was my agenda more important, correct, therapeutic? I think not. I realized, quite simply, I was jealous. The realization was salutary. I managed to return my attention to where it rightly belonged.

'You didn't talk?' I enquired.

'No,' she replied, a smile spreading across her face. 'You're forgetting the letter.'

'Ah, yes,' I said, well aware of the omission. 'The unopened letter.'

'It wasn't quite a letter,' she explained. 'It was a small envelope. Maybe that's what it had been in the dream, but that doesn't matter. When I got back from the loo, he'd disappeared. You'd have predicted I might have felt that familiar sense of disappointment, but I didn't. I just knew everything would be fine. And then I saw the envelope.'

'And this time you opened it?' I asked, now myself excited in anticipation.

'Yes,' she confirmed. 'His business card was inside with his name and telephone numbers – and a hand-written message. It said: 'We are such stuff … please call me'.

It transpired that the same evening she had called him. They had since spent the week together in what Cheryl described as 'magical bliss'. Of course, being realistic, it may not last. Like many instant attractions it may be doomed to failure. And surely Cheryl will need to grieve her lost father before she can create a real partnership with a man and not a dream prince – won't she?

But for now, having identified and tamed my own hidden emotion, I was pleased that Cheryl was basking in the pleasure of this man. I congratulated her and encouraged her to enjoy their meeting. As she got up to leave at the end of the session, I still had a remaining curiosity. She had mentioned the man's business card but not what his business was. As if she had read my mind, she turned in the doorway.

'By the way,' she said. 'He's a flying instructor.'

First Nature

There's a line in a song from *My Fair Lady* in which Professor Henry Higgins admits he's become accustomed to the presence of Eliza Dolittle to such an extent that he says 'her smiles, her frowns, her ups, her downs are second nature to me now, like breathing out and breathing in'. In the context of the song, it's a delightful sentiment. But it seems a strange simile to have chosen: surely breathing is a first nature necessity rather than a second nature habit. But I guess 'second nature' is used here as we commonly tend to use it to mean that something seems natural to us – despite the fact that we're really describing the opposite: an adaptation that's so successful it seems it's the reality (our first nature having become long since buried and forgotten). I believe it is this first nature that we, as psychotherapists, are helping our clients to recover and reclaim – to facilitate a more unadulterated self free from the necessary but now redundant adaptations of childhood – breathing deeply, freely and spontaneously from first nature rather than shallowly, carefully and in control, from our second nature. Perhaps psychotherapy is a bit like *My Fair Lady* in reverse – finding the authentic person of the flower-seller beneath the airs and graces of the Society Lady.

Sarah, my client, was not a society lady nor had she any pretensions of so being, but there was something equally unreal about her in how she presented herself. It was as if she wore an enormous Ascot hat of obsequious pleasing-ness totally obliterating who she was. Even on the phone, discussing a time and date for our initial meeting, she spoke as if it must be an awful nuisance for me to have to be making such an arrangement at all, assuring me that she could wait a few months, if that was more suitable. I could hear the wideness of her smiling mouth as she spoke and I was quickly aware of my irritated desire to wipe it off – a desire I was to experience many times in the course of our work together and which, for the most part, I was able to use helpfully (as information of how others might have treated her in the past), though I must admit there were times when my interventions, while delivered in a velvet glove, may have contained the intent of a hard slap.

Sarah was a slim, attractive, neatly dressed woman in her late-fifties, a wife and mother of five sons who, though each had long flown the nest, married and had children of their own, nonetheless seemed to demand a great deal of attention from her. Their father, Gerald, hadn't the slightest interest in them since realizing, very soon after their birth, that children are not like horses (of which he bred and raced several) in terms of independence, utility or financial gain. Sarah appeared at ease with this situation, implying that being 'covered' by her husband back in her twenties had been quite enough of that sort of thing and that his calling was more with the horses (and, I suspected, with several of the stable-girls) than the family. In many ways she'd been (and still was) the single mother of five sons. I doubt she'd had need of any monetary handouts, but in terms of practical, emotional and psychological support she'd managed to do without through what must have been difficult and lonely years. I was surprised at (though approving of) her decision not to have the children brought up, as she was, by nannies. It had meant her sacrificing any hopes of the artistic career she'd longed to pursue and, though she'd made a few friends (other mothers) over the school years, her life was mostly devoted to childrearing rather than socializing. She spoke of all this without a complaint or criticism but with a broad smile across her face throughout. 'Isn't life just wonderful?' it seemed to say. Pollyanna would have appeared pessimistic in comparison.

Sarah was embarking upon a one-year counselling course. Now that she had reached a certain age and with her children grown and gone, one might have hoped that she would now be looking to reclaim some of her own life, her artistic interests, her desire to travel to far-flung corners of the globe, perhaps to have a bit of fun, or even to enter therapy with a view to self-discovery. Not a bit of it. Her second nature would not hear of it. Sarah was seeking therapy because it was a requirement of the counselling course, the motivation for which was her desire to be of service to others in the selfless pursuit of their happiness. No, to be fair, she would not have put it like that. She would rather, with a wide smile, have said something like, 'I know I'll probably not be very good at it – but, in my own small way, maybe I can lend something of a helping hand in someone's less fortunate life.'

Sarah had several stock phrases in her second nature repertoire that would be scattered liberally throughout our sessions. Such self-effacing phrases as, 'Not wanting to blow my own trumpet ...' (before disclosing the tiniest feeling of satisfaction with her endeavours), 'I'm sure others are much more intelligent/skilful/wise/adept/creative/ etc.', 'Who am I to have an opinion/make a judgement/question things?' or, the *pièce de résistance*, 'Well, putting my feelings aside ...', in response to which I often wanted to say sarcastically, 'Yes, what have they got to do with anything?' but would choose the more kindly, 'What are these feelings you're putting aside?'

Helping people to change the beliefs they have developed over a lifetime can be a long and difficult process. They are, after all, and for all of us, part of our constructed identity. These beliefs are the nuts and bolts that psychotherapy attempts to undo and I'm not unfamiliar with some of them being rusty and hard to loosen. But Sarah's beliefs were more than rusty – a bit of lubricating insight wasn't going to move them – they were welded in place. By the time she had completed her year-long counselling course they were still immovably intact. Though, (un)naturally, she described the therapy as 'extremely helpful', I couldn't see that we had achieved much at all. I quite expected her to leave, her 'course requirement' having been met, but it seemed this was open for discussion.

'I'm sure you have many more interesting people to be working with,' began Sarah in her usual apologetic way, 'And I certainly don't want to take up a place for which someone more deserving might be waiting but I did wonder if you thought it might be helpful for me to stay in therapy a while longer. What would you advise?'

My thoughts were best kept to myself but went along the lines of, 'Can't you just hear yourself, woman? Stop being so apologetic about your very existence! If you want more therapy, go for it – just stop all this servile drivel!' But, though I said none of this, certainly not in that sort of way, the very fact I was thinking it but not expressing it helped me realize I was doing exactly what she was doing – I was being utterly inauthentic. I was being nice! Maybe the gloves needed to be removed. It was make or break time.

'Sarah,' I said, allowing a slight tone of honest irritation to enter my voice, 'in all this time, I have tried to explore and encourage the likelihood that beneath your benign, social presentation is an emotional, creative, passionate and articulate woman with desires and longings for a better future for herself. Now, with an obsequiousness of which Uriah Heep himself would be proud, you are asking me to advise you as to whether or not you should continue in therapy. What do *you* want?'

With these last four words I raised my voice almost to a shout. Sarah sat in stunned silence for a while but before long her face was full of movement. It was as if she was fighting back the obvious, the conditioned, the polite response which came to mind so easily and demanded to be spoken.

'I was going to say ...' she started.

'Then don't say it at all,' I put in abruptly, knowing it was likely to be something to do with wanting to be a good counsellor or a good mother or a good neighbour and something she'd already realized was not really what she wanted. 'What do you *want* to say?'

'I feel it too,' she said eventually, allowing her tears to roll down her cheeks. 'I feel there is so much of me buried inside – but I'm scared. I know there's more to me than this.'

I let her sit with her tears for a while, then asked gently, 'What are you scared of, Sarah?'

'I'm scared of letting it out,' she sobbed. 'I'm scared it will be too much, that once I take the lid off I won't be able to put it back on and I'll be out of control and crazy and angry and … and I don't know what.'

'Perhaps it's the "don't know what" that's the most scary?' I suggested.

'Yes, I'm frightened of the unknown,' she agreed, then went on, 'but I want to find out about it, I want to find me. And to do that, I want to continue here in my therapy with you.'

'Then that's agreed,' I said with a smile. 'It's great to hear you say what you want so clearly.'

I felt from this point on that Sarah was committed to herself. And, as a real person emerged in our work, I was more committed to her too. Our sessions became increasingly alive as she told her story with an honest expression of emotion. At this stage, this was predominantly sadness at the loss, when a young teenager, of her mother and a sense of meaninglessness in her life despite mothering her own sons and recently embarking on the counselling course (the practice of which she had wisely decided to delay until she had had more experience as a client). Through catharsis more than insight, those self-destructive beliefs that had seemed welded in place began to slowly shift, lubricated and loosened by her tears. Our relationship too developed dynamically as I responded to her more challengingly.

On one occasion I seem to have misheard her. I thought she was talking about one of her sons and I used his name in my next comment. She looked, at first, crest-fallen and I thought she was about to cry. I had no idea what about, as I hadn't ascertained the error on my part at this point. But soon her demeanour changed and she said with irritation, 'I'm not talking about Andrew. I'm talking about my husband. Why is it that you never listen to me!'

I was quite taken aback both by her anger and her global dismissal of my listening skills. I was convinced she had earlier mentioned her son by name. How could I have confused Andrew with his father, whose name was Gerald? Fortunately, I realized this was not the point. What mattered was that Sarah was expressing some anger towards me.

'You're angry that I never listen to you,' I simply reflected.

'Yes … well I was,' agreed Sarah. 'In that moment I was … I've lost it now and I know it wasn't a fair criticism. Of course, you listen to me. I sometimes wonder how you can bear to listen to …'

'Uh uh,' I interrupted, knowing she was about to revert to the old, self-effacing Sarah.

'Ah, yes, I haven't done that for a while,' she smiled. 'I was very angry. I could feel it welling up as soon as I realized that you'd thought I was talking about Andrew. Why does it matter? I'm not sure where I was going with moaning about Gerald anyway. But maybe that's the point. Gerald never listens.'

Much as I agreed with the connection she was making, I would have preferred her to stay with her anger with me and the dynamic that was unfolding between us so that she could work through some of her unexpressed aggression from the past. However, perhaps through fear, perhaps through her knowledge gained on the counselling course, she was not going to let this happen. Instead, she traced her anger back to its origins and circumvented the transference with: 'Of course, I married my father! Well, I had to. He made me. Two of the world's worst listeners – my father and Gerald! No wonder I felt so angry when I thought you weren't listening. It was like – here we go again!' She paused, then added, 'So just listen, will you?'

Though said with a teasing laugh, I noted the trace of anger still left in this last remark. Unfortunately, it was the end of the session but I had a feeling we would be returning to her anger at some future point.

Several weeks later, an opportunity for her anger arose quite by chance. I had just taken my month's summer break – a common enough time for clients to return feeling angry at being abandoned for so long. I doubted that Sarah had yet reached this stage in our relationship but fate helpfully intervened to up the ante. An accident on a remote country lane on my way back to my home prevented me from making it for Sarah's return appointment. I was not hurt but I was shaken by the impact of a car that had driven blindly out of a concealed entrance into my nearside door. Having phoned the police and left a message at home, I left a further message on Sarah's home number to say I had been unavoidably delayed and wouldn't make it back in time and apologized if my message was not received before she left. I suggested another appointment later in the week. But I did not hear from Sarah that week at all.

The following week she could barely look at me as she sat opposite me, breathing heavily and clearly fighting back her fury. I waited for some time before remarking, 'You seem to be holding back on what you want to say,' and a few silent moments later, having had no response, 'I think, understandably, you're angry about last week.'

Sarah sat as if in a trance, her body visibly trembling, her chest rising and falling as her lungs sucked in air and then expelled, in heavy sighs, some of her emotion, accompanied by a moaning sound. 'That bloody man!' she suddenly exclaimed. Stuck in my own train of thought, I assumed she was referring to me – voicing aloud some internal dialogue in the third person to avoid directing her anger straight at me. I was soon corrected.

'He took your message from the machine and didn't tell me!' she spat. 'That idiot "forgot" to tell me you'd called. I knew something was wrong when you weren't here. I knew you'd have tried to get through to me if you could but "No messages," he said when I got back. The fool even suggested I'd got it all wrong and you were still on holiday and, like an even greater fool, no, not a fool, like a trusting wife, I went along with him and decided I'd made a mistake. Until this morning, that is. This morning, Gerald, in passing, in his usual hurry to get to his bloody stables, told me you'd phoned after all. He told me you'd offered another time. It had just "slipped" his mind. Like hell it had. He just doesn't like me doing this. He doesn't like me doing anything I might enjoy! Well, he'll regret it one day. He'll learn how determined I am to have a life of my own … maybe even on my own.'

I don't think I'd heard Sarah talk for more than three sentences in a row before now. Neither had I heard her so angry. At this, I was both shocked and pleased. She was clearly changing and developing a stronger sense of herself and her own wants in life. This was surely the right direction but I wondered just how much of her anger with Gerald belonged also to me. I was not going to find out in this session. It continued with more expletives (all directed at Gerald) than I'd heard in all the weeks we'd worked together. No, her anger with me would not find expression for another few months and I was to be shocked by it even more.

'When you talk of your older brother, Jonathan,' I observed one day, 'you seem to almost worship him.'

'Well, he was *very* special,' Sarah responded, perhaps a little too emphatically. 'I don't think worship's the right word but I did adore him. I still do.' She sounded defensive. I decided to push a little.

'It's sometimes the case that we tend to adore the very thing we resent,' I stated, surprised at my complete lack of subtlety. I became even more obvious in my suggestion: 'The object of our hate has to be transformed somehow so that we can avoid our bad feelings which we fear might be destructive. I don't suppose he was perfect. He must have had his faults as an older brother?'

Sarah, having been reclining comfortably in the chair, uncrossed her legs and pushed her body forwards towards me. I thought she might be about to stand but, having set her feet firmly on the floor, she placed her hands upon her knees, arched her long back and raised her chin to face me squarely and solidly (reminding me, despite the difference in size, of a sumo wrestler sizing up the opponent). When she spoke, it was with a voice I hadn't heard before. I can only describe it as demonic.

'My brother,' she growled through clenched teeth, 'my darling brother is twice the man you'll ever be. Don't you dare find fault with Jonathan. Don't you dare to even suggest I feel anything but love for him. Just leave him alone!'

These last words were shouted loudly and I was much taken aback. Indeed, I was stunned into silence for what seemed like several minutes. I was scared and, in my fear, my thoughts were confused and unfocused. I knew I had to calm myself before making any response. I deepened my breathing to slow down my madly beating heart. Like Sarah, I planted my feet more firmly on the floor to ground myself. Only gradually did my faculty of thought return and I realized that my remarks had triggered some archaic state in Sarah, a state I believed was in response to her father but, having waited for so long for her to express her aggression at me, I needed for the moment to accept it – however frightening it was to be on the receiving end.

'Sarah,' I said as calmly as I could, attempting to control the shakiness of my voice. 'You are very angry with me right now. It seems important to me that you stay with what you are feeling … is there more you could say?'

Sarah remained in her aggressive posture, rigid, alert, her eyes darting from side to side as if vigilant for some attack. I could see her hands tighten as they gripped her knees, her knuckles white against her dark skirt.

'You bastard!' she yelled straight at me. 'You never liked Jonathan. You always picked on him. You couldn't stand that he was so wonderful – intelligent, athletic, creative, all the things you could never be! You were jealous! He so threatened your fragile sense of importance you tried to destroy him. Well, you didn't. You failed in that as you failed in so many things…'

'And with you?' I put in.

'You failed with all of us!' she persisted, her body heaving beneath the strength of her emotions. 'With Jonathan, with Susan, with mummy, everyone! You were a hopeless failure with everyone!'

'Including …' I began, but Sarah took over.

'Yes, me!' she wailed. 'Of course, me! Most of all me because I was the one who tried so hard to get it right. But you never listened to me … you didn't even see me. Despite the fact that I tried to be your good little girl, the quiet one, the polite one, the smiling one! You just couldn't be bothered. You were more interested in your horses and your money and your bits on the side. You weren't fit to be a father …. you were callous and cruel. You were a monster!'

'A monster you desperately tried to please …' I suggested.

'I tried so hard. I wanted you to show some love to me. I learnt how to fit in, to placate everyone, to make myself "nice" and obedient and helpful. All because I wanted you to value me but you never did. You hardly noticed me. I felt invisible, unwanted, like I should never have been born! If I hadn't had Jonathan to love me and protect me, especially after mummy died, I would never have survived. It was all a matter of survival, mere survival.'

'And now?' I asked.

'Now?' She looked me directly in the eye. 'Enough! No more! No more hiding myself away to please you, no more pleasantries or pretence. And if you don't like it – tough! Tough shit! You and Gerald and all those up-their-arses men ... well ... you can all ... you can all ... go fuck yourselves!'

Sarah remained still. Then, as if some demonic force, of a sudden, quit her body, she slumped back in the chair with a lengthy sigh. I sat in silence with her for a while. Her eyes were closed and I wondered whether she was, in fact, asleep. She looked very peaceful, the tension gone from her face, her body softly relaxed.

Just as suddenly, she was awake and sitting up and smiling. 'Well,' she laughed. 'That feels really good! I think I've turned a corner. I think I'm finding me at last. Thank you. Thank you so much.' And with that she walked gracefully and confidently to the door, looking like a new and vibrant woman. Maybe there was the touch of the flower-girl about her.

There were various opinions expressed by the members of my supervision group when I saw them that week but, despite their slightly differing theoretical slants, all of them considered Sarah's recent development as positive and constructive. I expressed some concern that she had seemed so different when she was expressing her anger, as if possessed by some demonic force, but was assured by the general consensus that such a level of repressed aggression, once released, would account for the dramatic nature of the catharsis. Her real self, one colleague suggested, would have needed such an enormous, energetic force in order to break through her rigid, lifetime's adaptation, it could not have been otherwise.

Over the next few weeks, Sarah continued to abreact. Though the content veered between childhood experiences with her father and her similar experiences as an adult with Gerald, her demonic aggression remained relentlessly directed at me – so much so that at times I feared she might at any moment lunge towards me and become physically violent. However, she never did and eventually I became accustomed to what seemed to become a ritual part of the sessions. She spent the initial period, before the growling, cathartic expression, describing the many changes she was making in her life. The idea of becoming a counsellor had long-since been jettisoned. She was now attending art classes at the local college. She convened a book club that met at her house on a weekly basis and she organized dinner parties and outings with the many friends she was swiftly making. Gerald objected furiously to the amount of time and money she was spending on herself and her friends but was given short shrift and told in no uncertain terms to 'get a life'. Her time for her children and grandchildren was drastically decreased but she enjoyed them more when she did have time to see them – her 'quality time' as she called it. She was no longer at their beck and call to run errands or baby-sit or sort out their problems – she was far too busy – and she was loving it. Her life was blossoming. She told of these developments with a lightness of voice and a sparkle in her eyes. Yet the intensity of her anger expressed towards me (in that strange state) during the latter part of our sessions did not abate.

Until last week, when, in our final session before the Easter break, there was an extraordinary change. She had told me of her exciting and busy week for the first half of the session, as she often did now, and after a few minutes' silence (a precursor to her cathartic release), she sat forward, placed her hands on her knees and drew breath.

'You bastard!' she tried – quite loudly but unmistakably in her own voice, her gentle, though these days more confident and assertive voice, not the deep, growling voice of a demon. As when it first appeared, I was quite taken aback – but this time by its remarkable absence. It was almost comical but I remained impassive as Sarah, looking slightly disconcerted, attempted again to say something to me. Nothing came. Her breath was released, her lips contorted to mouth some words but no sound emerged except the soft sigh of her exhalation. She looked totally bewildered. After several more attempts, she sat back.

'Well,' she said quietly after a while. 'There's nothing there. Do you think that's it?'

'What do you mean?' I asked.

'Has it all gone? Is that what happens? Is it like a reservoir with a finite amount of anger that eventually runs out?'

'Is that what it feels like to you?'

'Yes, it is. It feels like it's not even there for me to get in touch with. I'm not avoiding it – it just isn't there. Isn't that amazing!' She laughed delightedly.

'So how do you understand that?' I enquired, thinking it important to have some insight into the process – at least to try to understand it. I was curious to learn how she conceptualized what she had been doing for so long. I wasn't sure about my own perception of it and I certainly didn't understand the abrupt ending of such an energetic, emotional force. People usually go through a more gradual lessening of archaic affect than this seemed to indicate. I wasn't sure I trusted it.

'Oh gosh,' Sarah sighed. 'It's been such a journey, such a transformation! And I have you to thank for it. If it hadn't been for you, I'd never have got in touch with this part of me ... with all these feelings. My whole life has turned around because of this. I'm not sure I understand it, except I know that when I was in the trance ...'

'Ah!' I interjected. 'Is that how you see it?'

'Oh yes,' she affirmed. 'Definitely a trance. I could see you clearly, I knew I was talking to you but, at the same time, I knew I was really talking to my father, or Gerald – well, they're one and the same really! My anger towards them felt as if I was being taken over – from somewhere deep inside, there was a torrent of pent-up words and feelings that I just didn't know were there. They just demanded to be let out. And I did!'

'Yes, you did,' I agreed. 'You let them out very forcefully.'

'But you did know, didn't you, that none of it was to do with you?' She looked at me imploringly. 'Well, nothing and everything!'

'Nothing, and everything?' I echoed.

'Yes, nothing in the sense that any of my opinions and judgements were of you – but everything in the sense that you sat and listened patiently and without retaliation. You were like the father I didn't have, the one I should have had who could hear my anger and understand and still care about me.'

I felt very touched as she talked of her experience. She was describing (much more eloquently than 'therapy-speak' could) the reparative elements of the transference through which she had fought against her second nature and found her unexpressed self. Frightening though it had been for her to get in touch with that reservoir of deep and primitive aggression, she felt it was through her safe expression of it, and my acceptance, that she had now reached a point where she felt it was 'all emptied out' and she could get on with her life. It seemed to me our work might soon be drawing to a close.

'There's just one casualty in all this,' she put in just before the end of the session. 'You see, all that anger at my father, well that was from the past. He's been dead a long time. Now he doesn't exist psychologically either ... I feel I've said all I needed to say. I feel I've caught up with myself in relation to him. And, as a child, of course, I was trapped ... I couldn't get rid of him ... until now, of course, by coming here and working it through with you ... he's been totally obliterated. But Gerald ... well now ... Gerald is quite another matter.'

I was aware of the time. Only a few minutes remained and I had really wanted to devote them to asking about the Easter break and how she felt about it but there was something in Sarah's voice when she had talked of Gerald that concerned me: a slight deepening, a slight growling, a hint of that familiar, malevolent tone. I wanted her to know that I knew full well there was unfinished business that would need serious attention. Feeling unnerved and sounding emphatic, I said, 'This is clearly something we should address on your return.'

'Oh, yes. I'm sure we'll have lots to talk about after the break,' she laughed (though 'cackled' might describe it better) as her eyes darted wildly from side to side.

Chance Is a Fine Thing

The theme of the one-day conference was 'Serendipity'. I hadn't intended to go until Tessa, a dear friend and colleague, phoned serendipitously the previous evening to say she had decided at the last minute to attend and would be delighted if I would keep her company. Not having seen her for months, I agreed immediately and, putting down the phone after her call, retrieved the programme from the waste-basket to familiarize myself with some of the content that hadn't managed to attract me on earlier perusal.

Par for the course with such conferences, many of the workshops on offer made only tenuous links to the topic of serendipity. A few were more honest in not even attempting to pretend that serendipity concerned them in the least. Others seemed to be implying that serendipity had always been the cornerstone of their particular approach despite the differing impression they may have given at last year's conference entitled 'The Centrality of Goal-setting and Objectives' – but then, perhaps serendipity and opportunism may be close bedfellows.

Some of the workshops on the list had very long titles made up of multi-syllabic words, several parentheses and liberal sprinklings of Latin and Greek phrases in italics. Obviously they were following a school of thought that believes psychotherapy needs such obscure and convoluted description to justify its existence in an academic world. The workshops I was attracted to had more pithy titles such as 'Luck – can you make it happen?' or straightforwardly, 'What place has chance in psychotherapy?' or even more succinctly, 'Rolling dice'. They reminded me of that wonderful expression of Heidegger's – the 'thrown-ness' of life – and of my valuable experience many years ago when I was in therapy with an existential therapist. After prior years of therapeutic contracts, goals, targets, objectives and a relentless focus on change, I found it so refreshing when he would say at the end of each session, 'Well, let's see what happens, shall we?' And with that thought in mind, I gave up looking at the programme in favour of just that.

The next day, Tessa was in sparkling form when we met in the crowded foyer of the institute. She's a great one for telling jokes and anecdotal tales and, after our heartfelt greetings and enquiries were done, and tea and biscuits collected, she straightway launched into a hilarious account of a committee she had been on and the various unbelievable characters she had encountered. She was just telling me of the allergy-ridden chairman whose violent sneezing caused havoc with the ballot papers when I was tapped heavily on my shoulder from behind.

Now, one of the unfortunate consequences of having trainee therapists as psychotherapy clients is that meeting them at conference becomes an occupational hazard. It's one that can usually be handled by discussing the situation well in advance as well as addressing any thoughts and feelings afterwards. It's usually agreed that we will greet each other civilly and avoid attending any practical workshops where too much personal information may be disclosed or the confidentiality of our therapeutic relationship compromised. As I turned in response to the bludgeoning on my shoulder, I came face to face with Henrietta, a young, second-year therapy student and a client of mine who was, at the best of times, emotionally volatile and who at this moment, I could tell, was nearing eruption. It took a split second for her to explode.

'You lied!' she shrieked, causing several heads in the crowd to turn in unison in our direction. 'You told me you weren't going to be here. Well, that's a blatant lie! Here you are as large as life! I don't know that I can trust anything you say to me ever again!'

I turned back to Tessa who raised her eyes upwards with a sympathetically knowing expression as I excused myself.

'I think we need to find a quiet spot,' I said quietly, moving towards a corner of the foyer where I could see some space.

To my relief, Henrietta followed and I resumed, 'This is clearly very upsetting for you and I apologise for my unplanned presence ...'

'I asked you,' she interrupted in a loud mock whisper, eyes still blazing, 'I asked you only last week and you said you were definitely not coming. I don't know if I'd have come had I known.'

'It was unplanned,' I explained again. 'It was a last minute decision. Perhaps, I should have phoned you ...'

'Of course you should have phoned me,' she spat. 'What kind of a therapist are you that you just turn up out of the blue like this? Have you no sense of boundaries?' Given the hysterical, public display Henrietta was providing, the irony of this remark irritated me. I took a deep breath.

'Do you want me to leave?' I asked as calmly as I could, genuinely wanting to give her this option.

She looked astonished and for a moment I thought she was going to soften at my offer, but no, she was having none of it.

'Oh yes, right,' she hissed. 'You'd like that wouldn't you! Just so I'd be grateful for your sacrifice. You want me to feel guilty. Imagine how I'd feel knowing you'd left because of me. How could I ever face you again? You think you're being generous but I think you're just trying it on. Well, it's not working. You've totally ruined my day. You've really upset me, you have!'

'Henrietta,' I appealed. 'I am willing to leave. It's a very unfortunate situation and one which would have been much easier to handle had you known I was coming. What if I were to ...' but I could not finish my sentence.

'I'm leaving!' she shouted. Then, as she swept away into the throng, added sarcastically for all to hear, 'I hope you enjoy the bloody conference!'

I was feeling shell-shocked as I made my way back into the crowd to find Tessa, who helpfully waved to me as I fought my way, in a rather dazed state, through the mostly female gathering.

'Michael, you have such lovely friends,' she teased when I finally reached her. 'And I'll take a wild guess that she's a trainee therapist. But I know you probably can't comment.'

'No,' I replied. 'No comment. But it's not the best start to the day.'

'Not what you'd call serendipitous, I agree,' she said with a smile. 'Ah well, the day is just beginning. Who knows what's in store? What are you going to feast on next?'

'Feast? Oh, I see, um,' I took another bite of the rather dry biscuit I'd been holding all this time and glanced at the programme. 'I think I'll try the one entitled 'Chance is a fine thing'. It's the most interesting of the morning bunch, I think. Do you fancy it?'

'Looks interesting,' she agreed. 'But expedience prevails, I'm afraid. I just have to go and hear Professor Oakland's paper. He's supervising my doctorate and I desperately need the brownie points.'

'Oh, you mean the guy who's written a five line title, no words of one syllable and hardly a common English word among the classical Greek and Latin?'

'That's my man,' she laughed. 'It's going to be fun, fun, fun from beginning to end!'

'Good luck!' I chuckled, feeling much calmer now and able to put the earlier fracas behind me.

'See you at coffee,' said Tessa. 'Oh, and, Michael, don't go upsetting anyone else!'

After several wrong turnings in the rabbit warren of a building, I eventually found the right room, aptly more by luck than judgement, in which about thirty people were already, to my relief, sitting in rows, which meant I was able to slip into a seat at the back. The anorexic-looking young woman who welcomed us loudly and enthusiastically to her workshop had so much energy I felt instantly exhausted. Maybe I should have gone with Tessa to Professor Oakland but I was here now and I intended to make the most of it. And, to my surprise, Sonia, the slight but bright facilitator, woke me up and held my attention better than I'd expected. I was delighted that she did what many presenters fail to do: that is to define the subject from the start. For her purposes, she simply defined serendipity as 'the occurrence and development of events by chance in a happy or beneficial way'. I was happy with that. I also learned that the word originates from *Serendip*, a former name for Sri Lanka, and was coined in the eighteenth century by Horace Walpole in his fairy tale entitled *The Three Princes of Serendip* in which the heroes are constantly making fortunate discoveries. So far so good: just enough information to be interesting, not too much as to become overwhelming or tedious. Maybe this was a serendipitous choice? No, I mused, that must be a contradiction in terms. If I made a choice, it could not, therefore, be described as serendipitous. But what if my choice was a whim rather than an informed and determined act towards attending this particular workshop? Would that count? Could the mixture of choice and chance still be called serendipity?

I enjoyed my musing – for how long I'm not sure – but when the words 'experiential part of the workshop' gradually infiltrated my awareness, my heart sank. I should have read the programme more carefully. Audience participation is not my learning method of choice, well, not these days. Now I would much rather presenters played with their PowerPoints and projectors and allow me to ponder on things quietly. I thought to leave but already people were standing and moving their chairs to the back of the room right by the door beside me. It would have been too obvious and I certainly didn't want to offend Sonia, whose presentation, so far, I had enjoyed. I stacked my chair with the rest and stood awaiting further instruction as the clattering died away.

'Now, everyone!' shouted Sonia, clapping her hands for attention, 'I want you to find a space in the centre of the room and stretch your arms out and swing them wide to make sure you're not touching anyone.'

I was immediately transported back more than fifty years to my Primary School 'Music and Movement' class which was facilitated by the voice of an upper class man who, I am quite certain, spoke those exact words from a radio speaker in the hall. I prayed that Sonia was not going to play some music and ask us to move like a tree blowing in the wind. I was already wishing I had insisted on

my offer to Henrietta to leave but, dutifully, I milled about with
the others, found a space, and perfunctorily waved my arms about.
I could see I wasn't near enough to touch anyone without the arm
movement but it seemed the polite thing to do.

'Now, everyone,' said Sonia, lowering her voice in a conspiratorial
manner as she walked among us, 'I want you to close your eyes and
make a few turns.'

I half expected to hear Joyce Grenfell saying sternly, 'No, Michael,
not with your arms out – you'll crash into someone. What's that?
No, Michael, you are not a helicopter. Arms down!', amusing
myself with this thought, I turned several times making sure my
arms stayed by my side.

'Now stop – but keep your eyes closed!' shouted Sonia. 'In a
moment, I'm going to ask you to open your eyes and see who
is the first person you see and make some sort of contact with
them … all right, open your eyes now!'

There was a ripple of nervous laughter as we all opened our eyes.
Some had ended up facing the walls while others seemed to have
two or three people in view but I opened my eyes to find only
one young man's face smiling at me. He was very short and very
thin and had a little moustache that really didn't suit him tucked
under his nose. I smiled back and, while Sonia was organizing the
few for whom this 'chance meeting' had not quite worked out, we
moved nearer to each other.

'I'm Michael,' I said, as I held out my hand.

'Richard,' said the young man, shaking my hand rather damply.

'Now, introduce yourselves,' instructed Sonia, a little too late for us.

Richard and I continued to stand and smile.

'You've met this person,' continued Sonia, 'quite by chance. Some
may call it fate. Some may call it accidental. You might use the
words "coincidence" or "synchronicity". The question is – could
this meeting be serendipitous?'

Again several nervous chuckles – I could tell from their tone that
some had instantly decided that it couldn't. Others already knew
each other and made exaggerated moans implying that bad luck was
inevitable. I was already wondering what could be serendipitous

about my meeting with Richard. I was quite surprised at how wholeheartedly I was throwing myself into the experiment.

'Let's see what happens,' suggested Sonia. 'Take some time to get to know each other. Your task is to discover the positive in this meeting. Are there things you could learn from each other? Are there differences in your partner that might complement some of your qualities or skills? What is it about this chance meeting that could mean that serendipity is at play?'

Several couples crossed their legs, sank to the floor and began talking. Richard, without a hint of patronage, indicated a couple of chairs in a corner. I warmed to him enormously as I suspected he was quite capable of the full lotus position if he chose. I was even beginning to think maybe his moustache suited him in a Chaplin-esque, roguish sort of way.

' Shall I start?' he asked, leaning forwards eagerly and clasping his hands together.

'Go ahead,' I said, and leaned forward too in encouragement.

'Well, I'm 30 years old. I was born in Clapham – my parents are still there .... oh, er, and my brother. He's a year older than me. And I have a younger sister who lives in Darlington. I got married last year and we live in a flat in Highgate,' he began at speed, as if time was of the essence, but then just as quickly, he dried up. He was clearly not used to talking about himself.

'That's quite near me,' I offered, trying to find something in common. 'Islington, in fact.'

'Oh, just down the road then,' he replied.

'Yes, it is,' I said dully. I was beginning to feel this was hard work but, wanting to put him at his ease, I enquired. 'And are you in the therapy business?'

'No way,' he responded quite vehemently. 'I'm in retail.'

'So you're here because ...?'

'Oh, it's my wife. She's the therapist. Well, she's in training', he said with a tone of obvious disapproval, suddenly adding. 'They're all mad, these shrinks! They should be locked up, some of them!'

Suddenly, the rather benign Richard was turning into a snarling beast. His moustache took on a more Hitlerian aspect.

'Oh, that's a bit strong,' I asserted (though I agreed with him about the madness – it was the locking up I objected to). I was going to leap in to defend my profession from incarceration but then, deciding it was probably better to steer the conversation to steadier ground, I went on, 'I guess you're here with your wife then?'

'I was!' snapped Richard. 'She's left me here. Her stupid therapist stirred her up so much she had to leave. She says he only came to make her feel uncomfortable. What sort of a therapist would do that? My poor Henrietta … she's so sensitive and I think he's making her worse.'

'How awful,' was all I could manage to say. It was more a reflection on my current situation than a sympathetic response to what I'd just heard.

'How are we getting on?' asked Sonia appearing out of nowhere just in the nick of time. 'Are you finding the serendipity in your meeting?'

'No unfortunately we're not,' I said as I got up from my chair. 'But your appearance is fortuitous. You see, I've just remembered I promised to meet someone in the foyer about now and she'll be getting rather concerned if I'm not there to meet her … so, can I leave you with Richard? Perhaps, you could find some serendipity together – it's much more likely to happen between similar aged people, I'd have thought. But thank you for a most informative workshop. Unforgettable. Truly, unforgettable.'

Tessa was highly amused when, at the coffee break, she found me in a corner of the foyer skulking behind some potted palms and I described the workshop. I told her I'd just had another 'boundary situation'.

'It's not your day is it?' she said without any sympathy whatsoever. 'I wonder what's the opposite of serendipity? Sheer misfortune, maybe?'

'It's probably got a Greek name,' I grumbled. Even the coffee was tepid and tasted burnt. 'How's your workshop going?'

'Oh, it's all right,' she sighed. 'I don't think I'm cut out for academia though. It's all very serious and heavy.'

'Yes, well, you should have tried mine,' I moaned. 'I think yours would have seemed light-weight, and certainly safer.'

'So what are you going to do?' asked Tessa. 'I guess you're giving the second half a miss?'

'Yes I am, and you haven't exactly sold me on yours,' I replied. 'I think I'll stay here by the potted plants and read a book. Shall we have lunch out? I need to get out of here for a bit.'

'That would be great,' she enthused. 'I'll see you here at one. And, Michael ...'

'Yes?' I enquired, expecting to hear something about staying out of trouble.

'... things don't always happen in threes,' she said, laughing brightly.

But apparently they do. No sooner had I returned from the book stall with a few leaflets to browse through at my leisure, than someone dragged a chair over to my corner, *my* corner as I now very much saw it ... why to *my* corner? ... for heavens sake, there was a whole foyer full of chairs with no one occupying them!

'You're Michael Martin aren't you?' said an enquiring female voice. I raised my eyes to find a stocky, drably dressed, middle-aged woman peering at me intently. I thought to deny who I was but I had a sneaking feeling hers was a rhetorical question and I didn't want Henrietta's accusation to acquire any substantiation. For all I knew, this could be her mother come to shout at me.

'Why yes, I am,' I confessed. 'And you are?'

'Oh, you won't know me,' she insisted in a self-effacing way. 'I'm Maureen. I'm just an absolute fan of yours. I've read all your books. Gosh, I don't know how you find the time. Me, I've hardly time to do the laundry let alone write a book, ha, ha!' She had a laugh that held not a trace of pleasure. It was more of a strangulated cry of pain.

'Really?' I responded politely. Then, I don't know what possessed me, I added, 'A busy life then?'

'You don't know the half of it,' she said, but I just knew she was going to tell me.

An hour and a half later, having subjected me to the most excruciating details of her counselling work, her marriage, her family, her hobbies and her charitable work for the homeless (not to mention the intimate details of her gynaecological operations) she was about to launch into a developmental history of her childhood when, workshops over, the foyer began to fill with people. Thankfully, Tessa had not hung about to ingratiate herself with the professor.

'Ah, there you are,' she said to me as she joined us and, looking to my companion, added 'Hello.'

'This is Maureen. Maureen, Tessa.' I smiled as convincingly as I could. Though the phrase 'tedious monologue' was in my mind, I said, disingenuously, 'We've had a fascinating conversation.'

'Hello. Pleased to meet you,' said Maureen to Tessa. 'He's a one isn't he?'

'Oh yes,' agreed Tessa, looking completely nonplussed. 'He's definitely a one.'

'Are you going to lunch?' Maureen asked us both.

'Yes, we've decided to eat out,' said Tessa innocently. 'Were you thinking to eat here?'

'Well, I was going to ...' began Maureen.

'Such a good idea,' I inserted hastily. 'I'm told the canteen food is really excellent.'

'Ah yes, it is,' said Tessa, catching on quickly. 'We'd stay if we could but we have such a lot of important things to discuss.'

'Oh, I see,' said Maureen, looking crestfallen. 'Another time then? Maybe at the tea break?'

'Bye for now then,' I said noncommittally, feeling a real heel though not enough to change my mind. I took Tessa by the arm and we made for the door.

'My god,' she remarked as we stepped out into the street, breathing in a welcome bit of fresh air, 'you look ashen.'

'I feel exhausted,' I admitted. 'I couldn't stop her. She was like a demented word machine. She could filibuster for England. I just couldn't get a word in at all, not even to say I needed the loo. Imagine her working with clients!'

'Well, maybe she misunderstood the idea of "the talking cure"!' laughed Tessa, pulling me closer and hugging me. 'Come on, Eeyore, let's have lunch!'

'My treat,' I insisted, returning the hug. 'Thank heaven you're here!'

'Well, I don't think you'd have been if I wasn't.'

'True,' I chuckled. 'It's all your fault.'

We found a quiet little Italian place a few blocks away and, after a glass of Chianti and a bowl of delicious pasta, the world once more seemed soft and benign. It was good to catch up with Tessa. We've known each other since our early training days and shared a lot of ups and downs. She's one of those people who you feel you can share anything with and always receive an honest and thoughtful response. I know she feels the same about me and, having aired our current personal concerns about life, the universe and everything to our mutual satisfaction, we sat back to enjoy a decent cup of coffee before returning.

'I wonder if a conference on "Bad Luck and Malicious Meeting" would have meant you'd have had three lovely encounters by now,' mused Tessa. 'Maybe "Serendipity" is just tempting fate.'

'But you've been spared,' I pointed out. 'What have I done to deserve attack, slander and boredom in equal measure?'

'It must be your bad karma,' suggested Tessa. 'But *that* is about to change.'

'Oh, why's that then?' I enquired eagerly.

'Because you've offered to pay!' she teased. 'The gods will reward your kindness tenfold, I'm sure.'

'We'll see,' I said as I signalled the waiter for the bill and reached into my jacket. But, though I dug deep into every pocket, no wallet was to be found.

'I *know* I put it in my jacket,' I kept repeating, as moments later Tessa entered her PIN into the machine the waiter held. 'I put about a hundred pounds cash in it and I remember patting it to make sure just as I left the house. Oh hell, it must have dropped out somewhere on the way.'

'Stolen more likely, knowing your luck,' said Tessa unreassuringly. 'You'd better phone the police and cancel your cards.'

'I'm sorry,' I apologized. 'This was meant to be my treat.'

'You can pay next time,' she said. 'Your karma will just have to wait.'

'Serendipity, eh?' I sighed, taking out my mobile and switching it on. 'Is there such a thing?'

As I was about to dial, the first lines of 'La Vida Loca' (not an ironic choice of mine, I've just never discovered how to change the tone) jingled from my phone signalling a Voice Mail message. An unknown, Asian voice informed me that he had found my wallet and would be happy for me to collect it if I would care to phone. Tessa was delighted at the sudden turn around of events and that at least a smidgeon of good luck had come my way. She not only encouraged me to phone the man immediately but offered to drive me to his address. I made some protestations about her missing the conference on my account but she was insistent that she'd had more than enough of therapy-speak for one day and, in any case, she was happy to have gained her brownie points with Professor Oakland.

I must have dropped my wallet shortly after leaving that morning, as the address I'd been given was only a few blocks away from my home. We found it with no problem. Having promised her tea and cakes by the fire, I left Tessa waiting in the car while I ran up the steps of the old Victorian house and rang the bell. It wasn't long before the door opened and the delightful face of Mr Tharanga beamed down at me like a laughing Buddha, my wallet in his hand. Moments later, I was back at the car.

'We've been invited in for tea,' I told Tessa through the open car window. 'Mr Tharanga insists that he wants to meet you too. I think you'll love him!'

'Oh, okay,' she said, obviously bemused by the invitation. 'You seem very excited!'

'Well, I think it's such a good omen after all that's happened,' I laughed.

'Why?' she asked. 'I know you've got your wallet back but what's so funny?'

'It's Mr Tharanga,' I explained. 'He's such a delightful, hospitable, friendly man – and a psychoanalyst to boot – you'd think we'd known each other for years – but, most amazing of all, do you know where he's from?'

'I've no idea,' said Tessa.

'Sri Lanka!' I exclaimed.

Tessa looked puzzled. It took a while for the penny to drop.

'Serendip!' she laughed, eagerly jumping out of the car. 'Well, well, chance is a fine thing after all. I hope he gives us coconut cakes.'

Serendipitously, he did.

Unwrapping through discussion

I hope these short stories have been enjoyable for you to read simply as entertaining tales. Additionally, I hope you will enjoy 'unwrapping' them to discover how they may be helpful to you in your learning and reflection as a therapist. Each of the stories raises issues and challenges that might be faced by anyone preparing to engage, or already engaged, in the practice of counselling and psychotherapy. Maybe you have been critically assessing the style and interventions of the therapist as you have been reading each story and, as invited to do in the introduction, have been considering your own approach to these clients and the issues they present – in particular, identifying what you would have done or said differently. To assist your personal considerations and to stimulate discussion with your peers and colleagues, I draw attention below to some of the key challenges of each story and provide some questions for you to reflect upon from your own theoretical perspective. Where appropriate, I suggest further reading to explore these issues in more detail and refer to textbooks on specific theoretical and technical aspects in which you may be interested.

If there is one belief I have tried to convey in these stories, it is that there is no single 'right' way to work therapeutically with another person and that each unique dyad will find its own way to be together (perhaps, struggling to do so some of the time) for the benefit of the client.

The Carving

One of the issues raised in this story is the 'neutrality' of the consulting room and the private person of the therapist. Here, the therapist rationalizes the benefits of a neutral environment as allowing clients and their therapeutic relationship with him to be 'as unencumbered by extraneous intrusion or distraction as is possible'. The room is a 'background' to the relationship and the therapeutic work. It is an 'exploratory space' (p. 5). However, the story continues with descriptions of the various associations some of his clients make when a wooden carving is introduced into that space. The carving itself becomes a means of exploration of their fantasies and perceptions as well as a means of deflection.

- Do you believe the consulting room should – or could – be neutral or not?
- What for you might be the advantages or disadvantages of a neutral room?
- Do you agree with the therapist in this story that 'family photographs and personal memorabilia have no place here'. What might be the advantages or disadvantages of such things being present in the room?
- What's your opinion of the therapist's introducing the carving into the consulting room?
- What limits do you place upon yourself in terms of disclosure of your personal tastes and preferences to clients? What about details of your personal life? Are there occasions when sharing these might be appropriate? (In 'Not Playing It by the Book' the therapist discloses information about his father so we will be returning to the issue of self-disclosure again later.)
- Or do you attempt to be 'a blank screen'? To what end?

The client Deborah (p. 8) is an actor as well as a psychotherapist in training. Seeing the carving as a mask, she introduces the idea of a 'True' and 'False' self (Winnicott, 1965) in relation to her acting. The therapist challenges her by suggesting that her false self was not restricted to the stage but was present in their relationship and that it was hiding her real self away.

- What do you make of this intervention? It seems to work in this instance but what might have gone wrong? What are the risks?
- In suggesting Deborah talk directly to the carving/mask, what do you think the therapist intended by such a directive intervention?
- What do you think happens in this process of Deborah talking to the mask?
- How would you describe this process within your theoretical model?
- Is this way of working something you would do in your practice? Again, what are the risks involved?

You might like to explore 'experiments' as used in gestalt therapy (see Perls et al., 1951; Zinker, 1977; Sills et al., 1995; Mackewn, 1997; Joyce and Sills, 2010).

The adolescent client, Brian (p. 10), presents a conundrum for the therapist. It is unclear whether how he presents in the consulting room is as a result of his regular use of skunk in the recent past or other factors. Eventually, the therapist becomes convinced that Brian's apparent 'hallucinations' are a deflection from facing the realities of life.

- What would you be alert to when working with someone with a history of drug use?
- Do the therapist's doubts ring true for you?
- What might he have done differently to ascertain the possible effects of regular use of skunk?
- If you consider the therapist to have been accurate in his assessment, how, from your theoretical perspective, might you describe Brian's presentation? This could be in terms of formal diagnosis (such as that of the *Diagnostic and Statistical Manual of Mental Disorders*, DSM-IV) or a description employing concepts from your own theoretical model (transactional analysis, gestalt, psychodynamic, person centred, etc.).
- How would you distinguish your description or diagnosis from 'normal' adolescent development?

Subterranean

In this story, the client, Daniel, presents as an over-adapted, withdrawn and timid man who eventually begins to take small steps to becoming more confident and assertive. His therapist doesn't use the term, but could have described Daniel as someone with a 'schizoid' and 'avoidant' personality style. The therapist sees some positive development when Daniel appears to become, however slightly, more 'passive–aggressive'. The reader may be interested in learning more about such descriptions of personality adaptations, or character styles, in the literature. As useful introductions, I recommend the books of Johnson (1994), Benjamin (1966) and Joines and Stewart (2002).

- Do you concur with the therapist's view that Daniel's movement from compliance to mild rebellion is a positive one? Why?
- What might be problematic with this development?
- Have you experienced a similar process in the course of making changes yourself? What was that like for you? Did your shift from compliance to rebellion in the process of gaining confidence seem an inevitable step?
- What might have been another sequence in your, or Daniel's, move towards confidence and assertion?

At times the therapist is bored, frustrated, irritated and angry with Daniel's slow progress. At one point (p. 20) he says, 'I felt so far it was *I* who was feeling all the anger'. However, he does not overtly express these feelings to Daniel in case he might 'scare the little mouse back into his hole' (p. 21).

As well as not wanting to scare him, why else might the therapist have chosen not to share his feelings with Daniel?

- Can you think of situations with a client where you might share such feelings?
- What do you think the therapist meant by '*I* was feeling all the anger'?
- How would you describe the possible transference and countertransference (or other descriptions of relationship dynamics provided by your model) that is occurring here?
- In general, how would you describe the therapist's overall approach to Daniel?
- Does this fit with your approach or would you have worked differently. How?

Bion (1959) urged that we should be without memory and without desire when working with clients. Similarly, Lapworth and Sills (2010) write of staying 'creatively indifferent' (a term used in gestalt therapy). Yet in this story the therapist says, 'I believe the therapist sometimes needs to hold the hope the client is unable to dream of'.

- How do you understand these statements?
- What's your opinion? Do you subscribe to one or both of these views?
- If both, how would you explain the apparent contradiction?

When Daniel fails to appear for his session re-arranged at the new time, the therapist decides to phone him a quarter of an hour into the session (p. 26). He rationalizes this 'unusual thing to do' as 'showing his concern' and 'holding him in mind'.

- Would you have done the same?
- What reasons would you give for phoning or not phoning a client who had failed to turn up for their appointment?
- Do you have a hard and fast 'rule' concerning contacting clients outside of sessions?
- What might be the exceptions?
- What might be the therapeutic benefits or pitfalls of contacting clients in this way?
- Would you feel justified in phoning a client for your own convenience (i.e. to know whether or not to continue waiting)?
- If deciding not to phone, what would you do in the event of the client not appearing at the following session?

Holding Boundaries

The two previous stories have raised the issue of boundaries: the first in respect of the neutrality of the therapy room and the person of the therapist and, in the second, of making contact with clients outside the clinical setting. This third story presents as its central theme the boundary of confidentiality.

O'Brien and Houston (2007) provide a useful general summary of the concept of 'boundaries' that permeates therapists' language. They refer to the importance of stability – consistency and reliability – in treatment arrangements such as place, time, frequency, setting, role definition, fees and, most relevant to this story, confidentiality. They helpfully consider just why boundaries are important in therapy (which is sometimes easily forgotten when boundaries simply become a rule to follow) and they give a useful commentary, particularly applicable to 'Subterranean', on the potential unconscious dynamics on such occasions when the therapist changes the time or date of sessions. Jacobs (1988) and McLoughlin (1995) write of the importance of time and boundaries from a specifically psychodynamic perspective, while Clarkson (1995) writes of boundaries from a more integrative perspective and looks at some of the exceptions (or boundary breaks) that might occur within the therapeutic relationship. On this latter point, it is important to emphasize that 'ruptures' of the therapeutic boundary will happen. It is a rare therapist who does not take a holiday, need to alter an appointment time, increase fees or make some boundary error at some time – even making an 'outrageous intervention' (Pizer, 2005), which may cross the normally accepted boundary of the therapeutic relationship – however vigilant the therapist may be. Some would argue the necessity of such ruptures in the process of repairing relational deficits (see Mitchell and Aron, 1999; Stark, 1999; DeYoung, 2003; Maroda, 2004). What is vital is that the 'rupture' or 'enactment' be addressed, acknowledged and understood so that the relational experience becomes reparative rather than destructive. A strong working alliance (Gelso and Carter, 1985; Horvath and Greenberg, 1994) and a 'safe container' (Winnicott, 1965), need to be established as early as possible in the therapy in order to work through such ruptures at the therapeutic boundary. Confidentiality helps create this safe environment in which clients may explore the often hidden aspects of themselves.

- Why do you think boundaries – of setting, frequency, duration, confidentiality, endings, etc, – are important?
- What boundaries do you consider absolutely inviolate?

- When might you break the confidentiality of the client? How would you justify this?
- What does your own particular therapeutic model have to say about boundaries?
- What action would you take, and how would you explain it therapeutically, if:

  1 Your client persistently arrives late for their session?
  2 Your client fails to pay you for several weeks?
  3 Your potential client is the sibling of a previous client of yours?
  4 Your client is temporarily housebound and requests a home visit for their next session?
  5 Your distressed client asks you to hold them?

- In the story, the client, Helen, has a history of abandonment, physical and sexual abuse. What particular boundary considerations would you make in working with her?
- In an impulsive moment, the therapist asks his client, Lee, if he does salsa (p. 36), to discover if he has a connection with Helen. Why might this be 'totally out of order'?
- If Lee had wanted to know why the therapist asked such a question, how do you think the therapist could/should have responded?
- The supervisor (p. 37) seems quite clear that the therapist should hold the confidentiality of both his clients and not divulge that they are both in therapy with him and that he knows they are having a relationship. Given that congruence and authenticity on the part of the therapist are often emphasized as central to the therapeutic endeavour, how would you justify the withholding of this knowledge?
- What might have been the outcome of breaking confidentiality?
- How might you have dealt with the situation differently?

Not Playing It by the Book

There are several issues raised in this story, including another boundary issue, that of self-disclosure on the part of the therapist, which I will refer to later. The first challenge the therapist faces, however, is that of working with a student studying transactional analysis (Berne, 1969/81, 1972; Stewart and Joines, 1989; Lapworth and Sills, forthcoming). I chose a TA student simply because I have some knowledge of this model. The student could just as easily have been a client of any other model whether from the humanistic, psychodynamic or behavioural schools. Whether or not you are familiar with transactional analysis, the concepts referred to in the story are explained to the extent that the questions below will still be relevant to all readers. For those interested in learning of TA's development as a relational approach (p. 50) I recommend *Transactional Analysis: A Relational Perspective* (Hargaden and Sills, 2002) and *From Transactions to Relations* (Cornell and Hargaden, 2005). For those interested in the general movement within psychoanalysis and psychodynamic psychotherapies over the past few decades towards a more 'intersubjective' and 'relational' perspective, I recommend *Relational Theory and the Practice of Psychotherapy* (Wachtel, 2008), *Relationality: From Attachment to Intersubjectivity* (Mitchell, 2000) and *Psychoanalytic Treatment: An Intersubjective Approach* (Stolorow et al., 1987).

- If you are, or have been, a counselling or psychotherapy student and in therapy (as a course requirement or not), what was it like for you to be studying theory alongside your personal therapy?
- Was it important to you that the therapist was 'playing it by the book' (of your particular model) or not? Why?

Contracts are employed in many approaches to counselling and psychotherapy. The reader may wish to take a look at *Contracts in Counselling* (Sills (ed.), 2006) where Sills and others explore contracts and their applications from various perspectives. In the story, Mary seems to expect the therapist to make a treatment contract (p. 47) to which the therapist responds with some strong reservations.

- Do you agree or disagree with the therapist's reservations?
- What place do contracts (beyond practical arrangements) have in your model?
- What different types of contract might you employ with clients?
- What do you see as the advantages and disadvantages of contract making?
- What's your opinion on 'escape hatch closure' as mentioned in the story (p. 49)?

- Would you employ a 'no suicide' contract with a client and under what circumstances might you do so?
- When discussing the renunciation of committing suicide, homicide or going crazy, the therapist says, 'I don't want to preclude these options for myself' (p. 49). Do you? Why or why not? How might your views affect your work with clients?
- Would you make such a contract with your own therapist?

In the story, there then follow some incidents of self-disclosure. After a brief glimpse of some emotional reaction in Mary's face (p. 51), the therapist attempts to respond to her differently. However, he is soon feeling frustrated and, in response to her challenge, gives his honest opinion of her via the theoretical construct of her Parent ego state (p. 51).

- Whether you use the term Parent ego state, introject, internalized object or another term with which you are more familiar, what is your understanding of what is being described here?
- How do you respond to the therapist openly describing Mary as 'cold, angry and extremely critical' (p. 51). What are your views on such an intervention?
- How in your model would you conceptualize what is happening when the therapist realizes he was 'becoming the very Parent ego state I was describing'?
- Having made a breakthrough when Mary expresses sadness (p. 52), the therapist is 'prepared for the backlash in the next session'. Why do you think he was prepared for this? How would you describe Mary's possible internal dynamics which may bring about the backlash?
- When Mary asks 'Was your father as smug as you?' the therapist ponders on several responses he could have made (p. 53). What response might you have made and what would have been your intention in such a response?
- The therapist chooses to disclose information about his father, describing him as not smug (as in Mary's accusation) but a very gentle and modest man. Why is such disclosure on the part of the therapist not 'a perfectly straightforward and innocuous thing to say' (p. 53)?
- A little later, he makes the further disclosure that his father died when he was 7 years old. His rationale is that it felt relevant and right. What

do you make of this? Is there justification in a therapist doing
something because it simply feels right? What are the pros and cons
in acting on intuition or 'gut feelings'?
- How, in your model, would you describe the changing overt and
  covert dynamics occurring between the therapist and Mary throughout this story?

In at the Deep End

Trust is the central theme here and though (for the sake of the
story's drama) there is an ironic turning of tables, I hope it highlights
well enough the importance of trust on the parts of both client and
therapist. I hope it also emphasizes the need for discrimination in
trust – sometimes taking an informed risk and sometimes having
what might be called a 'healthy paranoia' – without which we may
find ourselves 'in at the deep end' or only able to 'hover about at
the shallow end' (p. 57) of life.

Even prior to attending a therapy session, the need for trust in
the ethicality and professionalism of counselling and psychotherapy
is going to play a part in clients' turning to a therapist. Recent
moves to go beyond existing registration with professional bodies
(e.g. BPS, BACP, UKCP) towards government regulation of the
psychological therapies have been developing in an attempt to
protect the public and inspire their trust in therapy.

- Do you think that regulation will help public trust in the counselling
  and psychotherapy profession? Why or why not?
- How might regulation have the opposite effect?
- In what way do you think the public's trust might be inspired?
- How might you promote yourself as a trustworthy, ethical and profes-
  sional therapist as you are starting, or maintaining, your practice?
- When looking for a therapist yourself, what would help assure you
  that you can trust a particular therapist?

Most approaches to therapy stress the importance of the 'working
alliance' (see Gelso and Carter, 1985; Horvath and Greenberg, 1994;

Clarkson, 1995) in the building of which trust plays a central part. Conversely and additionally, through the working alliance further trust is established, assisted by agreement on goals, concordance regarding tasks and the development of personal bonds between therapist and client (Bordin, 1979).

- What personal qualities as a therapist do you consider will facilitate your clients' trust?
- What other aspects of your practice will help the establishment and maintenance of trust?
- What assisted you in trusting your own counsellor or psychotherapist?
- Were there times when you had doubts in your therapist? Why and what could have been done to redress this?
- In the story, how does the therapist work with Pauline to inspire her trust?
- At one point, the session is interrupted by the doorbell ringing (p. 61) and eventually the therapist goes to answer it. How do you respond to the therapist's handling of this break in the therapeutic boundary?
- How might you have handled the situation differently?

Pauline's 'paranoia' is apparent throughout the story. (See personality adaptations or character styles in Johnson (1994), Benjamin (1966) and Joines and Stewart (2002).)

- How would you define the term 'paranoia'?
- Which of Pauline's behaviours would indicate to you a paranoid adaptation?
- How do you understand the aetiology of paranoid thinking and behaviour within your model?
- What is your understanding of the psychodynamics that may be occurring when the therapist starts to show paranoid thinking and behaviour in relation to Pauline's mother?
- It is only towards the end of the story (p. 70) that the therapist's suspicions turn from the mother to Pauline, by which time Pauline has left the therapy. But if, earlier in the work, he had been unable to trust the truth of what Pauline was presenting, what could he have done?
- How important is it that you trust and accept all that your clients are telling you?

- How might you handle a situation where your trust in your client's authenticity is in question?
- There are several occasions in the story when the therapist chooses not to comment on some of the incidents that occur within or outside the therapy sessions. Reading of his increasing stress and anxieties, you may feel you can excuse him in the context of this story. However, how would you handle the situation and what would be your rationale for doing so in situations when:

  1 Your client uses your first name (p. 64) for the first time or unexpectedly uses a term of endearment towards you?
  2 You suspect your client is becoming sexually attracted to you (p. 65)?
  3 You receive a letter from a hostile relative (p. 66) of your client expressing opinions of both you and your client.
  4 You receive a phone call from a concerned friend or relative asking for information about the work you are doing with your client.

- Further, would you:

  1 Leave a message on your client's telephone answer-machine (p. 63)?
  2 Inform your client of the reason for cancelling a session (p. 63)? With how much detail?
  3 Work with a client who had turned up at the wrong time and you had time to see them (p. 64)?
  4 Accept your client suddenly announcing taking a break from therapy (p. 68)? Why or why not?

High Spirits

In this story, the beliefs of the therapist and those of his client, Luke, are very much at odds. The therapist is not convinced by what Luke describes as a problem of being 'spiritually lost and incomplete'. Rather, following his 'rule of thumb', the therapist suspects underlying sexual issues.

- How do you respond to the therapist's 'rule of thumb' and his application of it in this story?
- How would you have worked differently with a client presenting with similar 'spiritual' issues?

- How does your model describe the redirection of energy (sexual or psychological) towards another aim or object?
- Though he realizes he is 'pompously wedded' to his theory (p. 72), the therapist persists in applying it. If you were his supervisor, what questions might you want to ask him?
- How does the therapist's attitude and behaviour in this story square (or not) with your personal and professional, ethical position? (You might like to refer to the BACP's Ethical Framework (www.bacp.co.uk/ethical_framework) to assist your discussion.)

People with a variety of spiritual, religious, cultural and political beliefs will appear in our consulting rooms and we as therapists may strive to meet them with unconditional positive regard, a non-judgemental attitude and congruence (Rogers, 1990/1957). But when our own beliefs are in conflict with our clients' beliefs, maintaining these core conditions is not an easy task. How might you respond to clients who:

1 Consider that women should play a subservient role to men?
2 Believe that contraception is a sin and condemn others' use of condoms even in areas where HIV/Aids is widespread?
3 Use homophobic, racist or misogynistic language in the session?
4 Request that you pray, chant, meditate or perform a shamanic ritual with them during a session?
5 Believe that their god or higher power or karma or astrological chart accounts for their situation?
6 Ask you to share your religious or political views?

- At one point Luke's therapist considered 'referring him on to someone more on his wavelength' but Luke 'seemed the more determined that I was the right therapist for him' (p. 75). In a similar situation, would you consider referring on a client to someone else you thought more compatible? If your client was determined to stay with you, would you agree or insist on another therapist? Why?
- Having learned of Luke's abusive treatment by his mother, the therapist says 'The cruelties parents inflict upon their children, in my opinion, are unforgivable' (p. 78). Are you in agreement with this statement or not? If you learned of the abusive background of the client's parents (and, in all probability, *their* parents) would this affect your view?

- What, for you, is the place of forgiveness in therapy?
- Do you see your clients' forgiveness of abusive parents as important in the healing process when working with traumatized clients? Either way, are there exceptions?
- In light of the therapist, at the end of the story, having an experience that was 'sexual and simultaneously … "spiritual"', do you think he should share his experience with Luke? What might be the outcome of such a disclosure? Would you have shared it?

Some approaches to psychotherapy explicitly contain a spiritual or transpersonal element (my colleague, Charlotte Sills, considers them to be ubiquitous enough to be seen as a 'Fourth Force' in the world of psychological therapies, alongside psychoanalytic, humanistic and behavioural forces). For those interested in this fourth dimension, I recommend *Psychosynthesis* (Assagioli, 1975), *Zen Therapy* (Brazier, (1995) and *Mindfulness Approaches to Psychotherapy* (Baer, 2006) as useful introductions, and, of course, the many relevant papers in *The Collected Works of C. G. Jung* (1970/1958).

The Audition

Central to this story of a film-star client who wants to 'say goodbye' to her father is the employment of the 'empty chair' technique from gestalt therapy (Perls et al., 1951; Sills et al., 1995; Mackewn, 1997; Joyce and Sills, 2010). It is used in this instance as an experiment to help Heather, the client, get in touch with and express her blocked feelings (p. 87). The therapist suggests she talks to her father, imagining him sitting in the vacant chair by means of which Heather finds an authentic voice to express her rage, her sadness and her love: in other words, her grief.

- What do you think are the advantages and disadvantages of the use of this technique?
- Do you agree with this therapist's rationale for using it with his client? Why?
- In what circumstances might you consider using the empty chair technique in working with a client. How, in your model, would you explain the dynamics of this experiment?

- Apart from imagining a person in the empty chair, how else might you use it?
- This technique is sometime referred to as 'two-chair work' where the client is invited to move from one chair to the other and create a dialogue as they alternate between the two. Similarly, several chairs may be employed. How might this be useful?
- In what circumstances might you use these variations of the technique for yourself?
- In the story, Heather is a film star of whom the therapist has no prior knowledge and is unaware of her fame. Why might this be blissful ignorance?
- What might have been the potential difficulties had he recognized her and known her as a famous person? And what might be the disadvantages of not recognizing the celebrity of a client?
- It becomes apparent towards the end of the story that the therapist has disclosed his client's fame to his supervision group (p. 92). Would you have done the same? Why or why not? What level of client confidentiality do you think is important in supervision?
- Do you feel critical of the therapist agreeing to work with this client despite the six-month time constraint and the nature of the work (p. 85)? Why?
- Do you think there is a case for taking on clients when we feel 'excited', 'seduced' or challenged by them (p. 85 and 86)? How might this be problematic? How might this enhance the therapy?

In the final session of this short-term therapy, the therapist and client spend some time summarizing the work and acknowledging each other's participation (p. 89).

- Do you consider this to be important when ending with clients? Why?
- What else do you consider important when dealing with the end of therapy?
- What would you do differently if you were ending with a client after several years of therapy?
- As a client, what have your experiences of therapeutic endings been like?
- In retrospect, is there anything you would have done differently?
- What's your opinion on the following:

  1 Lessening the frequency of meeting en route to the end of therapy?
  2 Devising together an ending ritual?

3 Exchanging cards or gifts at the end of the work (or even after the end of the work)?

4 Being available to the client should they want to return in the future?

Dream On

True to its title, the theme of this story is a dream. It follows two possible ways of interpreting the same dream's symbols and finding meaning: one being prophetic (the romantic client's wish fulfilment), the other the unconscious resolution of early loss and grief (the 'realistic' therapist's preferred understanding). In the event, though the therapist's interpretation seems to be a potentially useful one, the symbolism of the dream turns out to be prophetic.

The prophetic qualities of dreams have probably existed throughout history. Dreams as the 'royal road' to understanding unconscious processes, particularly wish fulfilment, came in the late 19th century when Freud first published his work *The Interpretation of Dreams*. Jung in the early 20th century perceived dreams, informed by the collective unconscious, as a form of psychic regulation brought about by access to all that is repressed, neglected or unknown. For those interested in Freud's and Jung's thoughts on dreams, I recommend Freud's *The Interpretation of Dreams* (2001) and *On Dreams* (2001) and Jung's *Dreams* (2001) and *Memories, Dreams, Reflections* (1995).

- What are your thoughts on dreams? Do you think they are:

  1 Prophetic?
  2 Resolving past repressed, neglected or unknown issues?
  3 Simply 'junk' left over from the day's events?
  4 'Communal' or shared by others?
  5 Integrating disowned or 'split off' parts of oneself?

- Have you had experience of dreams that would support your view of each or any of these?
- In the story, the client and therapist refer to the dream in the present rather than the past tense (p. 97). What might be the advantage of this?

- What's your view of the therapist questioning Cheryl at each point of the dream? What do you think he is facilitating by doing this?
- How else might he have facilitated his client through the dream? (For a gestalt approach to dream-work, see Mackewn, 1997; Joyce and Sills, 2010.)
- What do you understand by the client's reference to her 'masculine and feminine aspects' (p. 98) and how does your model conceptualize these aspects?
- How might you use them in your therapeutic work with clients?
- Would you have explored Cheryl's 'round the bend' Freudian slip in her telling of the dream (p. 99) or, as the therapist did, would you have joined in the laughter? Why?
- Do you subscribe to the view that dream symbols have direct correlation to specific meanings (for example, Cheryl's assumption that a therapist would interpret 'snakes as sexual symbols, phalluses' on p. 100)?
- What might be the advantages or disadvantages of such a 'dream dictionary' approach?
- How does your model's theory encompass dreams and how does it suggest working with them?
- If you had a dream that involved your client, would you share it with them? Why?
- Throughout the story, there is a discrepancy between Cheryl's 'romantic' optimism and the therapist's 'realistic' pessimism and between Cheryl's view of the dream as 'saying something positive' and the therapist's perception of it as a means of grieving the early loss of her father.
- What do you think of the therapist's handling of this discrepant situation?
- What would you have done differently?

First Nature

This story is based upon the idea that our 'first nature' (our unadulterated self) becomes subsumed under our adaptive and compromising 'second nature' in the course of growing up, and that the task of therapy is to discover and free the authentic person beneath these adaptations. Most developmental theories subscribe to this idea, describing such adaptation in terms of the formation of a 'False Self' (Winnicott, 1965), 'internal working model' (Bowlby, 1969), 'life script' (Berne, 1972), or 'organizing principles' (Stolorow et al., 1994) and so on.

- From your theoretical perspective, what word or phrase might encapsulate this adapted self?
- How does your model describe the formation, development and maintenance of this 'second nature'?
- What therapeutic processes or techniques might you employ in facilitating the emergence of a person's 'first nature' self?
- Rogers (1990/1957) suggests that the 'core conditions' of unconditional positive regard, empathic understanding and the therapist's congruence are necessary and sufficient to facilitate self-actualization. Do you agree? What else do you consider might be necessary?
- How centrally do you place the therapeutic relationship in this process of change and how do you explain its importance?
- To Sarah's rather servile, 'please others' adaptation the therapist responds, at least internally, with irritation, even wanting to wipe the smile off her face (p. 106). Assuming the therapist is not usually an aggressive person, how do you understand this dynamic theoretically? The therapist suggests one possibility of what might be occurring here, potentially providing him with useful information. What other possibilities are there?
- How might you handle your own feelings – anger, sadness, fear or delight – in response to a client?
- Do you think it might be appropriate to share them – in what circumstances, how and to what purpose?
- What's your opinion of Sarah's motivation to train as a counsellor being to 'lend something of a helping hand in someone's less fortunate life' (p. 107)?
- Do you consider it a sound motivation? Why or why not?
- If you are a counsellor or psychotherapist, what is or was your motivation to enter training? What do you see as the originating and reinforcing influences of your choice?
- What's your take on the idea of the 'Wounded Healer'?
- What influenced you towards your choice of your particular model?
- Later (p. 108), with some forceful interventions (comparing her to the obsequious Uriah Heep, telling her not to say what she is about to

say), the therapist challenges Sarah to express what she wants. How do you respond to these interactions?

- What are the pros and cons of this 'authenticity' on the part of the therapist?
- What might you have done differently?
- Sarah begins to loosen her self-destructive beliefs through 'catharsis rather than insight' (p. 109). What does this mean to you and how might you explain this from your theoretical perspective?
- How else might you intervene to challenge and change negative self-beliefs?

Central to this story, change occurs through the dynamics of the relationship between therapist and client – often referred to as the transference and countertransference. For those interested in exploring these concepts further, I would recommend Freud's (1935) seminal work *A General Introduction to Psychoanalysis*, Clarkson's (1995) integrative and comprehensive overview in *The Therapeutic Relationship* and Lapworth and Sills' (2010) 2nd edition of *Integration in Counselling and Psychotherapy* where an updated relational view of these dynamics in psychotherapy can be found.

- Your own model of therapy will likely have its own terminology for these projective (and introjective) dynamics. Relating them to the story's development of the therapeutic relationship, how would you describe the interactions that take place between the therapist and his client?
- How do you see the part played by the therapist's errors and absence?
- Would you, like the supervision group, consider these developments as 'positive and constructive' (p. 114)? Why?
- How might you have handled such eventualities differently?

Chance Is a Fine Thing

Concluding this collection, this story takes a light–hearted, tongue–in–cheek look at the role of chance and serendipity in the life of the therapist. It also brings us back full circle to the issue of boundaries. Early on in the story, the therapist refers to Heidegger's expression 'the thrown-ness' of life. According to Cohn (1997), 'this points at the limits of our control over existence' and the fact that many situations in life are not chosen. He and other existential writers emphasize that though this limitation is a given, and cannot be changed, our response to it (as to our past history) can. Readers may be interested in existential approaches to therapy and I would recommend Yalom's (1980) *Existential Psychotherapy*, Cohn's (1997) *Existential Thought and Therapeutic Practice* and van Deurzen-Smith's (2001) *Existential Counselling in Practice*.

- How do you view 'chance' and the 'thrown-ness' of life, and incorporate it as part of your therapeutic approach and practice?
- Similarly, how do you integrate other existential givens such as freedom, death, separateness and meaninglessness within your approach and practice?
- The existential therapist mentioned in the story, rather than setting objectives and having 'a relentless focus on change', ends each session with 'Well let's see what happens, shall we?' (p. 120). What is your reaction to this?
- Do you consider this an appropriate attitude? How do you see it as being useful or not?
- In the story the therapist, on meeting his client at the conference, says he will leave (p. 121). What else could he have done?
- In explaining that his attendance was a last minute decision, he says perhaps he should have phoned his client. Should he have done? Why?
- If you met one of your clients by chance outside of the therapy setting how would you handle the situation?
- What agreements might you put in place prior to this eventuality that might help the situation?
- Would you make differing allowances, and what might they be, if you met your client:

  1 At a party or other social event?
  2 At a weekly choir or yoga class?
  3 At a funeral?
  4 In a local supermarket?

- How would you handle meeting a friend or relative of your client in these same situations?
- Imagine accidentally meeting your own therapist outside of the therapy room. What might that be like for you and how would you like your therapist to behave?

By the way, if you see me at a conference – or anywhere else for that matter – and you aren't a client of mine (in which case, we'll know what to do), please come and have a chat.

References

Assagioli, R. (1975) *Psychosynthesis*. London: Turnstone.

Baer, R.A. (2006) *Mindfulness Approaches to Psychotherapy*. Burlington, MA: Elsevier.

Benjamin, L.S. (1966) *Interpersonal Diagnosis and the Treatment of Personality Disorders*. New York: Guilford.

Berne, E. (1969/1981) *Transactional Analysis in Psychotherapy*. London: Souvenir.

Berne, E. (1972) *What Do You Say After You Say Hello?* New York: Bantam.

Bion, W.R. (1959) *Experiences in Groups*. New York: Basic Books.

Bordin, E.S. (1979) 'The generalizability of the psychoanalytic concept of the working alliance', *Psychotherapy Research and Practice*, 16: 252–60.

Bowlby, J (1969) *Attachment and Loss* (Vol. 1: *Attachment*). New York: Basic Books.

Brazier, D. (1995) *Zen Therapy*. London: Constable.

Clarkson, P. (1995) *The Therapeutic Relationship in Psychoanalysis, Counselling and Psychotherapy*. London: Whurr.

Cohn, H.W. (1997) *Existential Thought and Therapeutic Practice*. London: Sage.

Cornell, W.F. and Hargaden, H. (2005) *From Transactions to Relations: The Emergence of a Relational Tradition in Transactional Analysis*. Oxfordshire: Haddon Press Ltd.

DeYoung, P.A. (2003) *Relational Psychotherapy: A Primer*. New York: Brunner–Routledge.

Freud, S. (1935) *A General Introduction to Psychoanalysis*. New York: Liveright.

Freud, S. (2001) 'The Interpretation of Dreams' Pt 1. In *The Complete Psychological Works of Sigmund Freud, Volume 4*. London: Vintage.

Freud, S. (2001) 'The Interpretation of Dreams' Pt 2, and 'On Dreams'. In *The Complete Psychological Works of Sigmund Freud, Volume 5*. London: Vintage.

Gelso, C.J. and Carter, J.A. (1985) 'The relationship in counselling and psychotherapy: components, consequences and theoretical antecedents', *Counselling Psychologist*, 13 (2): 155–243.

Hargaden, H. and Sills, C. (2002) *Transactional Analysis: A Relational Perspective*. Hove, East Sussex: Brunner–Routledge.

Horvath, A.O. and Greenberg, L. (1994) *The Working Alliance: Theory, Research and Practice*. Chichester: Wiley.

Jacobs, M. (1988) *Psychodynamic Counselling in Action*. London: Sage.

Johnson, S. (1994) *Character Styles*. New York and London: Norton.

Joines, V. and Stewart, I. (2002) *Personality Adaptations*. Nottingham and Chapel Hill: Lifespace Publishing.

Joyce, P. and Sills, C. (2010) *Skills in Gestalt Counselling and Psychotherapy*, 2nd edn. London: Sage.

Jung, C.G. (1970/1958) *The Collected Works of C.G. Jung*. London: Routledge and Kegan Paul.

Jung, C.G. (1995) *Memories, Dreams, Reflections*. London: Fontana Press.

Jung, C.G. (2001) *Dreams (Routledge Classics)*. London: Routledge.

Lapworth, P. and Sills, C. (2010) *Integration in Counselling and Psychotherpy*, 2nd edn. London: Sage.

Lapworth, P. and Sills, C. (forthcoming) *An Introduction to Transactional Analysis*. London: Sage.

Mackewn, J. (1997) *Developing Gestalt Counselling*. London: Sage.

Maroda, K.J. (2004) *The Power of Countertransference: Innovations in Analytic Technique*. Hillsdale, NJ: The Analytic Press.

McLoughlin, B. (1995) *Developing Psychodynamic Counselling*. London: Sage.

Mitchell, S.A. (2000) *Relationality: From Attachment to Intersubjectivity*. Hillsdale, NJ: The Analytic Press.

Mitchell, S.A. and Aron, L. (eds) (1999) *Relational Psychoanalysis – The Emergence of a Tradition*. Hillsdale, NJ: The Analytic Press.

O'Brien, M. and Houston, G. (2007) *Integrative Therapy: A Practitioner's Guide*. London: Sage.

Perls, F.S., Hefferline, R. and Goodman, P. (1951) *Gestalt Therapy*. The Julian Press; reprinted 1972 London: Souvenir Press.

Pizer, B. (2005) 'Eva get the goldfish bowl: affect and intuition in the analytic relationship'. Invited paper presentation at the Toronto Institute for Contemporary Psychoanalysis.

Rogers, C. (1990/1957) 'The necessary and sufficient conditions of therapeutic personality change', *Journal of Consulting Psychology*, 21 (2): 95–103.

Sills, C. (ed.) (2006) *Contracts in Counselling*, 2nd edn. London: Sage.

Sills, C., Fish, S. and Lapworth, P. (1995) *Gestalt Counselling*. Bicester: Speechmark Publishing.

Stark, M. (1999) *Modes of Therapeutic Action*. Northvale, NJ: Jason Aronsen.

Stewart, I. and Joines, V. (1989) *TA Today*. Nottingham: Lifespace.

Stolorow, R.D., Brandchaft, B. and Atwood, G.E. (1987) *Psychoanalytic Treatment: An Intersubjective Approach*. Hillsdale, NJ: Psychoanalytic Press.

Stolorow, R.D., Brandchaft, B. and Atwood, G.E. (eds) (1994) *The Intersubjective Perspective*. New Jersey and London: Jason Aronson.

van Deurzen-Smith, E. (2001) *Existential Counselling in Practice*. London: Sage.

Wachtel, P.L. (2008) *Relational Theory and the Practice of Psychotherapy*. New York: Guilford.

Winnicott, D.W. (1965) *The Maturational Process and the Facilitating Environment*. London: Hogarth.

Yalom, I. (1980) *Existential Psychotherapy*. New York: Basic.

Zinker, J. (1977) *Creative Process in Gestalt Therapy*. New York: Brunner/ Mazel.